Disclaimer and Permissions

This book is for informational purposes only. Although the author and publisher have made every effort to ensure that the information in this book was correct at press time, the author and publisher do not assume and hereby disclaim any liability to any party for any loss, damage, or disruption caused by errors or omissions, whether such errors or omissions result from negligence, accident, or any other cause. The advice and strategies contained herein may not be suitable for your situation. You should consult with a professional where appropriate. Neither the publisher nor author shall be liable for any loss of profit or any other commercial damages, including but not limited to special, incidental, consequential, or other damages.

No part of this publication may be reproduced, distributed, stored in a retrieval system, or transmitted in any form or by any means, including photocopying, recording, or other electronic or mechanical methods, without the prior written permission of the author, except in the case of brief quotations embodied in critical reviews and certain other noncommercial uses permitted by copyright law.

TO MY BOYS

Table of Contents

Introduction

If you're like me, you face both the joys *and* the challenges of parenthood. Maybe you're fed up with your child's outbursts and wonder how many tantrums are too many. You want to address his behavior with empathy and patience rather than through punishment. You want to lessen fighting as well as equip your child with the skills to prevent arguments in the first place.

You've tried time-outs. Counting to three before they're *really* in trouble. Maybe you've lost your temper. Except nothing is working, at least in the long run. You continue to butt heads—and you're exhausted with having to deal with yet another day of disciplining.

And here's why: we've got this discipline thing all wrong. We assume discipline is about punishment, or we assume it's what we need to take away from them to curb misbehavior. We mistakenly believe that the main purpose of discipline is to stop tantrums and outbursts at all costs, as quickly as possible.

Let's get to the real definition of discipline: discipline is teaching our kids.

Because isn't that what parenting really is? Our job is to arm them with the skills they need and would serve them well in the future so they grow into kind adults who can regulate emotions or empathize with others. They'll be adults who treat others with respect and don't expect the world to bow down to their wishes. The kind of person you'd want your child to eventually grow up to be.

With each outburst comes the opportunity to help them develop these skills. They learn more about their feelings and appropriate ways to express them. A child who can articulate "mad" can identify that emotion and use techniques to convey frustration.

Introduction

So that next time, there won't *be* a tantrum to get their point across but rather a more mature discussion or a different way to control their temper.

And the best way to discipline is through connection. As ironic as it sounds, we need to connect with our kids when they're acting up. The times when they're most unpleasant are when they need us the most. Connection works to prevent outbursts as well as better handle them when they inevitably happen.

This doesn't mean you'll be permissive. You still need to enforce limits and set boundaries. You won't let your child continue to jump on the couch or color on the walls when he's not allowed to. But you focus on what you want your child to learn from the incident rather than only making sure he doesn't do it again. Because yes, it's important your child stops coloring the walls. But it's equally important for him to develop the skills to communicate and make better decisions. You don't accept the behavior, but you are there to guide him through it.

I'll be honest: I hesitated writing a parenting book. I'm a regular mom. I don't hold a PhD in child development. I've never taught in a classroom. And other than with my own kids, I don't spend time with children regularly.

So where did I get the idea to write a book? It started with a blog.

I began Sleeping Should Be Easy (sleepingshouldbeeasy.com) in 2010 as an online journal about being a mom. I recorded milestones, described outings, and most importantly, I wrote parenting lessons.

The blog gained momentum and resonated with other parents going through the same things. Many wrote to me, saying that posts I'd written helped them handle their own conflict with their kids.

Others admitted they felt frustrated with parenting and found answers to their problems in my blog. Friends in my 'real life' who read the blog came to me with questions, looking for advice. You can say it was my readers who prompted me to write a book, both those who explicitly said I should and those whose readership let me know I was onto something. If they found my words useful, then maybe others will too.

Does this mean my kids are always well-behaved and I'm super mom? Far from it. Just like you, I have my bad days. I still lose my temper. I'm not always on my A-game. The same goes with all three of my kids. We all have had (and will continue to have) terrible days. And I'll be the first to admit this parenting thing is tough. Don't be surprised if you catch me losing my cool with my kids once in a while. (Just ask my family!)

But I've seen how certain approaches have yielded more effective results. And I feel more confident with the way I raise my kids, even as I'm still learning new ways to go about it.

One of the main lessons I learned is this: there's no one-size-fits-all solution. I often wrote on my blog, "Do what works for you." *You* know your child, yourself, and that particular situation far better than me or anyone else.

And I think that's why my blog resonates with so many people. You are still the expert with your child, regardless of the struggles you may have. You simply need the tools that work best for him.

Part one of *Parenting with Purpose* outlines preventative measures and how we can create a parent-child relationship that minimizes the potential of conflict.

In part two, we discuss effective ways to handle outbursts and standoffs while still relying on a solid connection between you and your child.

Introduction

Part three talks about the aftermath of conflict or, as I like to think, where the real lessons of parenting happen.

And finally, the book's bonus chapter includes 20 actionable items you can do to put these tips into practice.

This book provides you with the tools you need to handle conflict as you see fit. What worked one day may not work the next. And what worked for your first child may be ineffective with your second. You don't have to get it "just right." Instead, your primary goal is to define what you want to teach your child, and how to use connection to do so.

No matter where you are with your child, this book will strengthen your relationship with him. While you'll never love a tantrum, you'll learn how to handle them. You'll deal with *fewer* outbursts because you taught your child how to regulate himself. You'll raise a child who not only behaves most of the time, but one who *wants* to.

And you'll begin to enjoy the time you spend with your child much, much more.

Don't waste another day fighting or yelling. Raise well-behaved kids, prevent tantrums, handle conflict and build a strong parent-child relationship. It begins with prevention.

PART ONE

PREVENT MISBEHAVIOR THROUGH CONNECTION

Chapter 1

Connect with Your Child to Reduce and Prevent Conflict

You don't know what to do anymore. Every week, sometimes every *day*, you and your child have some sort of conflict. Another tantrum your toddler is having. You go through a standoff with your six-year-old about not wanting to go to the grocery store. Or maybe your child throws a fit because she wants to read with you but you can't—you still have dinner to prepare. Never mind you're exhausted from just having come home from work. She empties the box of Lego all over the floor. She follows you around the house, whining and crying. Now, not only is dinner late, you also have to deal with a frustrated child.

Day in, day out.

You've tried common advice like time-outs, counting to three, spanking. But nothing seems to work.

If this sounds familiar, you're not alone. Many parents struggle with daily conflicts with their kids. They dread coming home from work or face a new day only to have another fiasco with the kids. Every day there seems to be yet another challenge that runs counter to the supposed joy of parenthood.

But don't worry: you can strengthen your relationship with your child. You can build respect for one another, and learn how to parent calmly without losing your temper.

How? By connecting with your child.

Connection prevents tantrums, builds your relationship with your child, and lessens conflict. Connection happens both during peaceful days as well as right when you're in the thick of another struggle. In fact, connection is even more important during your child's tantrums and standoffs.

Practical Ideas for Connecting With Your Child

Let's back up a minute and talk about how to prevent outbursts through connection. Let's say you've come home from that exhausting commute from work. But rather than diving into your household tasks or shooing her away, you connect with your child first.

When you first see your child wants attention, light your face up with a smile that says: "I'm so glad to see you." Each time you're with her, make a habit of giving her a genuine hug and kiss and express how glad you are to see her.

At first glance, this approach doesn't seem to make sense. There's so much to do. You're tired, and you just want to change into comfortable clothes or at least use the bathroom. But you've noticed your child being extra clingy at this time of the day. You've shooed her away too often in the past to realize that doing so isn't working.

Instead, connect with your child, even if it seems like it can wait. Set aside distractions and spend as little as a few seconds to give her a warm hug and kiss, or a couple minutes reading a book, devoting every moment only to her. This routine will stop her from nagging and misbehaving to get your attention; when you fill her bucket first and recharge her batteries with your attention, she'll be much more willing to play quietly nearby while you get changed or prepare dinner.

At home, I've learned to connect with my kids each time I see them. The initial 'reunion,' whether from picking them up from school or giving a hug when I get home or even when we wake up in the morning, may be brief. But they're genuine and not distracted. For as little as five minutes, I give my kids my full attention. Sometimes I sit them on my lap or listen to their day at school. I don't wipe the table or rearrange the books in the shelves. I make sure I am all theirs.

" YOU ARE YOUR CHILD'S FUEL."

Think of it this way: you are your child's fuel. When you've been apart or when you have a habit of not giving her your full attention, her fuel will be running low. You need to replenish her attention fuel even for just a few minutes so she can continue with her day. But you have to give genuine, heartfelt attention with no distractions. Once she's topped off, then she can better play on her own. You can then use this time to do whatever tasks you needed to do.

Implementing this habit has prevented so many outbursts. I don't rush through everything I need to get done while shooing the kids away "until later." I focus on them first, and then get to the tasks later. Because we've reconnected, they feel more confident going about their day independently. I can cook while they play nearby. We can clean up toys together in peace. We've already started off on the right foot, and conflict is less likely to occur.

Chapter 1

Balancing Your Life and Theirs

This isn't a call to drop everything—especially time-sensitive tasks—for your kids, however. Clearly if you can't read a book because your hands are coated with breadcrumbs from the kitchen, your child has to wait. But generally, you want to start your day by acknowledging her in a genuine, heartwarming way. Doing otherwise makes her feel left out and empty.

Another approach to connecting with your child when you can't drop everything is to invite her to "help." If you need to change into more comfortable clothes when you get home, ask her to help put your shirt into the hamper. Stand her on a chair so she can watch you cook. You can then combine your everyday tasks and chores with spending time with your child.

Similarly, remove distractions when you're with your kids. Here's my confession time: However good I am about not being on my computer with the kids, I can be downright hypocritical with smart phones (which, really, is just a mini-computer). I'll check my email while trying to hold conversations with my kids or hop on Pinterest while the kids are playing nearby. I've even told them to wait just a minute until I finished something unimportant on my phone.

Recently, I decided to stash the phone in my bedroom, far away from where I can sneak a peek while I'm with the kids. Even "What if my husband is trying to call me?!" excuses aren't good enough (he can reach me on the landline). It's no surprise that I feel more productive and connected on the days when the phone is far away.

Maybe your distraction is also your phone, or the television, or even blaring music. Maybe your pile of work is clouding your mind with its pressing needs. Maybe you're preoccupied with other worries, or even exciting plans you can't stop thinking about. Maybe chores and tasks that need to get done around the house are often on the forefront of your mind.

This isn't a bad thing, but there's a time for them. And preferably not when you're supposed to be engaging with your kids. This isn't to say you devote 100% of your time to your kids and save everything else for when they're asleep. In fact, I advise the opposite: when appropriate, do chores and tasks *with your kids*. They'll learn the values of doing chores as well as how to actually do them. You'll also free up your time so you're not overwhelmed in the evenings.

When you're paying attention, you should be able to tell when some things have crossed the line into distractions. Your child isn't part of the equation, for example. Perhaps you're hoping she can play with her blocks alone just a little bit longer so you can respond to an email. Meanwhile, she's hammering for attention, needing you at that moment. And she somehow picks the most inconvenient time to show you her latest craft or tell you the color of the fire truck. Listening to your child is difficult when you're doing something else.

When possible, give your child your full attention, even if only for a few minutes. It'll take less time to stop what you're doing than to multitask and frustrate her (which will only frustrate you as well). With fewer distractions, you're present with and listening to her. You won't have to deal with the ensuing whining or attention-getting shenanigans, either.

Try to avoid the typical "uh-huh" response we parents sometimes give when our kids are talking to us. If it really isn't possible to listen to her, let her know. "I'm trying to park the car right now, but once we're done we can talk, okay?"

" CONNECT WITH YOUR CHILD SO
THESE OUTBURSTS DON'T HAPPEN SO OFTEN. "

The more you coerce, beg or punish, the bigger your disconnection with your child. Rather than resorting to a quick fix ("Here, play with this toy for now") or worse, losing your temper, connect with your child so these outbursts don't happen so often. When you reunite with her, such as after school or when she wakes up, greet her with a genuine hug and kiss. Be glad to see her, and make sure she knows you enjoy and value her company.

Spend as little as five to ten minutes focusing on your child. If it can't wait, explain that you'll be with her as soon as possible, and stick to your word. The more you do this, the less likely she'll nag you in the first place.

Connecting and listening to your child keeps her from resorting to tantrums to get your attention in the first place. When you meet her needs, not only will she not whine or nag, but she'll also feel respected and loved and will treat you the same in return. Your relationship will improve dramatically when you remove the extra distractions in your day and focus on your child.

In the next chapter, we'll talk about one of the main reasons we need to focus on our kids without distractions: respect.

Chapter 2

Respect: Give It to Get It

You're wondering where you went wrong that your child thinks it's okay to talk back. The worst is when he acts disrespectful to other kids and adults as well. You're shocked at some of the phrases coming out of his mouth. Especially when, not too long ago, he was the sweetest and kindest person.

You've tried everything. Taking his beloved toys away, time-outs, no television, spanking. Your little boy still talks back, disrespects others and isn't pleasant to anyone.

As harsh as it may be to say, the first place to look for answers is you. When your child disrespects you, reflect on your own actions to see whether they are setting a precedent. When we discuss disrespectful kids, we look at the behavior in isolation, or as a one-sided thing. But the improvements in our children often begin with us changing our behaviors as parents.

You need to give respect to get it back, including with your child. He can't treat you well if you don't model respect yourself.

And this doesn't apply to just our kids either. How do you treat your loved ones, from your spouse to your family and friends? Do you gossip about others, then wonder why your child was mean to his friend the same way? Do you yell, lose your temper and act just as disrespectfully as your child?

Staying calm and mature is difficult, even over the smallest discrepancies. Our kids spill a cup of water and we get upset as if spilled water is the worst thing in the world. Never mind that we would never react that way had an adult spilled that same cup of water. Our kids deserve the respect we would give another adult.

One time, I was disciplining one of my twins when my five-year-old said, "You don't have to say it mean." Even he understood that while my intentions were good, I didn't need to be a jerk about it. I realized my mistake and asked for a do-over where we discussed his behavior in a more respectful manner.

Managing Strong-Willed Children

How do you know if you're having a power struggle with your strong-willed child? You know you have a power struggle when you're determined to *win*.

Being strong-willed isn't a bad thing. Your child is motivated and reaches for what he wants. He's a natural leader. He doesn't succumb to peer pressure. His independent and self-sufficient spirit drives him to want to do things for himself.

But some of these positive traits can test parents with a different agenda. Strong-willed children want to be in charge and will test limits. They're *passionate*. Imagine the two-year-old who wants to "me do it!" as he fumbles with putting on his shoes while mom waits nearby knowing he's not quite there yet.

We adults can sometimes take this power thing to a whole new level. Because of our role as parent, we forget we're dealing with other human beings. We disrespect our kids in ways we wouldn't other adults or our partners.

Honoring Your Child's Feelings

Sometimes, acting disrespectfully to our children isn't so obvious. You may assume your actions are positive, but they instead contribute to his disrespectful actions.

For instance, parents may not know they're dismissing their child's emotions. Here's a typical example I've been guilty of many times: I tell my kids "It's okay," or "It's just a toy—we can get another one," or "Don't be scared."

Brushing aside your child's emotions makes him feel unimportant, and that his feelings remain unheard and aren't as valid as someone else's. Instead, acknowledge his emotions without judging them as petty or insignificant. Fighting with a school friend (even if we know they'll likely make up the next day) feels just as real to him as it would to you in a similar situation with one of your friends.

Instead, listen without judging. You want to build a relationship with your child where he can tell you *anything* and you would still support him no matter what. That can only happen when you allow your child to talk without judging his thoughts or actions. Don't call his dreams silly or go on and on about a mistake or accident he made. In fact, *thank* your child for telling you the truth even if it means he's in trouble. He was brave enough to tell you the truth and admit his faults when he could have easily kept the truth from you to avoid punishment.

And avoid teasing your child or laughing at his expense. We adults take this too far sometimes. Our kids do the cutest and funniest things, but often not on purpose. Teasing, laughing at them or sharing a funny story behind their back can feel disrespectful.

The other day my five-year-old mentioned, "Did you know I have a girlfriend?"

Surprised, I caught myself and didn't tease or make a fuss out of it like I know some families do ("Oooooh... you have a *giiiirrrllfriend!*"). Instead, I reacted in the same way I would hear another one of his pleasant tidbits about school. "Oh, I didn't know. Tell me about her—what's her name?"

My son doesn't even understand the true meaning of boyfriends and girlfriends. The last thing I wanted was for him to wonder why his mom is teasing him. Or worse, decide from then on to keep his mouth shut next time. As with most cases when considering children's feelings, I picture how *I* would feel if I were in his shoes.

Another way we might unintentionally disrespect our kids? By being condescending. We often speak to our kids at their level—simplifying words, eliminating complex concepts, even speaking slowly so they comprehend our words—but sometimes we take it too far and talk down to them. We talk to them as though they couldn't understand if we spoke normally. We continue "teaching" and explaining every little detail when they would rather observe or figure things out on their own.

Just as importantly, accept your child for who he is. We don't make our kids. They are their own person. The quicker we recognize and cherish this, the better we'll be at accepting who they are. Embrace your son's introversion, however difficult it may be for your extroverted self to relate to him sometimes. Don't pressure your son to excel in sports when he would rather play music. Get to know your child, and celebrate his personality. Unfair expectations can prevent your child from shining in the ways he feels comfortable.

Respect Your Child's "No"

Speaking rudely or yelling at our kids are blatant signs we disrespect them. But what about other ways we do so unintentionally?

Particularly, not obliging our kids when they say "no." We tickle them when they've already made it clear they want us to stop. We force them to give up toys and share with others when they're not done playing yet. Sometimes we disrespect our kids in the most unlikely moments.

It's easy to overlook our kids' "no," like asking incessant questions when they've already said "no." Still, it's important we listen and respect their limits for the following reasons:

You teach your child that he has boundaries.
Stop when your child asks you stop, especially with tickling or pestering them even in jest. Otherwise, you invade his personal space and send the wrong message that adults can simply tickle or annoy him with little regard to his feelings.

You let your child know that he has a voice.
Stopping when your child asked you sends the message that you value and consider his words. While you have the authority, he also learns that he has a voice. Parents and adults aren't always right.

You encourage your child to stand up for what's important to him.
Kids who are encouraged to say "no" when they're playing with a toy will learn how to stand up for what's important to them. Today it may be a toy, tomorrow it can be their personal values, a job promotion they deserve, or a passion they want to pursue.

★

It all comes back to us, the parents. Start fresh and respect your child as you would any other adult. When he sees and feels your genuine respect, he'll return that back to you. Honor your child's feelings and don't dismiss them too quickly. And respect your child's "no," as doing so teaches him valuable lessons like standing up for himself.

Chapter 2 - Respect: Give It to Get It

Give respect to get it. The more you respect your child, the better your relationship with him will be.

Chapter 3

Set High Expectations to See Results

You want your child to behave well without so much nagging on your part, but she doesn't seem to make significant changes and instead reverts to previous behavior. You're scared you're destined to raise a misbehaving child until she moves out of the house.

But the problem is you've got an image of your child as someone who misbehaves. You've branded her as someone who won't or can't change. You've set low expectations, and she has more than met them.

The power of expectation is strong with children. How do you view your child? Do you pick up after her and let her talk back because you figure that's just how she is? Or do you expect her to behave, to be self-sufficient, and to respect others?

Define your expectations... then enforce them. Your child has the potential to meet your expectations. Kids who misbehave do so because they've heard that's all they're capable of. Your expectations of your child will influence her effort and view of herself.

How can you reset your expectations so you start with a clean slate? How do you convey this message so your child knows what's expected of her? And how can you use high expectations to encourage positive behavior?

Start with a Clean Slate

Your child's behavior up to this point is a result of what she has been accustomed to. She didn't wake up this morning behaving the way she does out of the blue. Instead, she's grown used to certain messages and certain ways of life that enabled her behavior to continue the way it has.

While temperament influences how we act, by no means are we born the way we are, destined for a certain path of life. Our life circumstances and upbringing also influence much of how we've acted up to this point.

The same goes for your child. Her temperament may lend itself to misbehavior. But guidance also shapes much of how she acts. This is by no means a guilt trip of what you could've or should've done. Rather, it's a reminder that you're not stuck at all. We can do many things to promote behavior we want while reducing the ones we don't.

Maybe you have three kids, and one of them misbehaves more than the others. Have you branded her as the "troublesome one"? Avoid the unfortunate consequences of labeling your kids with supposedly innate traits. Children aren't "good kids" or "bad kids."

For instance, saying, "You're always misbehaving!" or "Why do you give me so much trouble all the time?" establishes expectations that lead to misbehavior and trouble-making. Those negative expectations will be pretty hard for your child not to live up to, especially if she hears it often.

Instead, start with a clean slate. Don't let your child's past skew your view of her or change your opinion. Discipline is teaching. Understand your child's impulses and connect with her. Then show her the right way to behave in a loving environment.

Praise Positive Behavior

Kids thrive on attention, whether good or bad. And unfortunately, arguments, yelling, and scolding are a type of attention they'd rather have than none at all.

The best way to counter misbehavior is to praise your child and give her attention when she is behaving. Maybe you saw her treating her little brother kindly. Point that out and say, "It looks like you made your brother happy when you shared the blocks with him." Or give her a high-five and observe that she put her dishes in the sink after dinner, all without you asking.

Kids want to please their parents. They want our approval and are crushed when we seem disappointed or angry with them. Use that to your advantage and praise your child when she behaves well.

Smart parenting advice tells us not to praise character-based traits (e.g. "You're so smart!") and instead praise the effort ("You must have studied so hard!").

This is true about effort-based traits like one's smartness, athleticism, artistry and such. You wouldn't want your child to think her good grades are inherent and have nothing to do with effort. This would only make her shy away from anything difficult that might label her as "not smart." Nor do we want our kids to feel locked in to a certain talent, such as implying she's the artistic one while her brother is the athletic one.

Behavior and values, however, are different.

In this case, you would want your child to believe kindness and good behavior are inherent. Saying "You're so kind," would bear more impact than "You did a kind thing."

Say phrases like, "You made your sister happy" after she shares toys with her brother. Or "You are so loving and patient" after she behaves well with others. In praising her character, you're saying she's a good, well-behaved child.

Give your Child Responsibilities

Trust is placed when giving responsibilities. Not only do you entrust your child to do the task correctly, you also send the message that you expect her to do so.

Give your child new responsibilities appropriate for her age and skill level. Maybe she needs to put breakable dishes on the kitchen counter all by herself. Brushing her teeth with no help. Helping you carry a bag of groceries into your home. Convey your belief that she can succeed and meet your expectations.

Entrust her with new responsibilities and set the bar higher. By giving her tasks that are a notch above what she's used to, you've set your expectations high.

Erase the mindset of a misbehaving child and establish new and higher expectations that demand respect, kindness, and love. Set expectations that warrant praise for hard work and good behavior. Expect nothing less than the kind of adult you would want your child to grow up to be.

After all, low expectations equal low performance. Your child isn't going to surprise you out of the blue by behaving well when you don't expect her to.

Instead, set high expectations, and treat your child the way you want her to behave. Hold *all* your children accountable whether you believe one misbehaves more than the other or not.

Change your mindset, and you'll notice a huge difference with how your child behaves. She will live up to your expectations, whether they're set high or low. The higher you set your expectations of good behavior, the more likely she will meet them.

Chapter 4

The Importance of Routine

It's 7am. I open the door to the kids' bedroom, wish them a good morning and hand the little ones their milk. They'll usually say, "Open curtains and blinds. Turn off fan. Turn on light." They expect all this because we do the same thing every morning. Little rituals dot our whole day, from putting toys away at the end of the day to placing clothes into the hamper before bath times. Even our daily flow has a rhythm that relies on a general structure—a template that we fill in.

My kids have thrown tantrums because life feels a little chaotic and they don't like it one bit, but having routines helps turn chaos into calm with them. When changes disrupt our normal flow, the routines lessen potential tantrums and offers familiarity.

> **"ROUTINE DOESN'T MEAN BEING INFLEXIBLE TO LIFE'S CIRCUMSTANCES."**

Before we get into the benefits of routine, let's discuss what routine is *not*: Routine doesn't mean being inflexible to life's circumstances. While consistency is key, rigidity is not.

Instead, routine is doing many of the same things throughout your day. Life remains predictable so your child knows what happens next.

Create daily routines such as washing hands after every meal and taking a bath at 7pm every night. Create a general *structure* of your day, such as sticking to a 12pm naptime.

With that in mind, why are routines important?

The Benefits of Routines

Routines keep you on schedule.
Some of the reasons children act up, whine or throw tantrums are because their basic needs aren't met. Your child may be complaining about a broken toy, but beneath the outburst is a sleepy child who needs a nap. Or maybe he has gone too long without eating. Or he needs your attention.

Routines make sure you take care of your family's basic needs. Having breakfast every morning ensures your child isn't hungry in a few hours. Napping in the early afternoon every day keeps him happy and healthy into the evening. Reading bedtime stories fulfills his needs to bond and spend time with you.

Routines quell hunger, tiredness and the desire for company, all on automatic. You prevent outbursts when your child is well fed, well rested, and nourished both physically and mentally.

Routines encourage self-initiation.
Reminding your child over and over to do something isn't pleasant. With routine, you don't have to: he knows exactly what to do. Without reminders, he knows to take off his shoes when he comes home. He puts dishes away right after eating, and he heads straight to the bathroom to wash his hands.

Without a consistent routine, your child won't know what to do. Rather than run on automatic, he has to think about whether he's supposed to go straight to the bathroom or take his shoes off first.

Routines get rid of the time-consuming tasks of discerning what to do next and instead encourage his self-initiation.

And as your child grows, you especially want him to initiate responsibilities and do things on his own. Eventually he'll go to school or spend less time with you. Raising a self-sufficient child starts with implementing routines.

Routines lessen power struggles.

Remember when I mentioned that routine is your new best friend? That's because routines do the parenting work for you. You don't need to nag to get the next task done. Your child won't throw a tantrum at the park when you say you're heading home for lunch. These are activities he expects as normal because you do them all the time. He won't question every decision you make or assume you've decided to leave the park because you're being a "mean mommy."

Routines lessen anxiety.

Anxiety: We all deal with it to varying degrees. And when you're a child, anxiety is heightened by the fact that you're not even aware of the emotions flooding through your mind and body. Anxiety can happen any time, but some common culprits include new environments and people, a change of plans, a disruption of routine, or a separation from the familiar.

Routines prepare your child for what's coming up so not everything is brand new. With a clear set of expectations, he is better able to overcome anxiety, especially to new events, experiences, and people.

Routines also lessen the fears or anxiety your child may have while you're out and about. If you're taking a family trip, you can rely on your regular routine to reassure him that all is well. You might be in a different city, but you can still implement the same nap and bedtimes, for instance. The familiarity of your standby routines calms him enough to enjoy the trip rather than worry or miss being away from home.

Kids thrive on predictability. They don't like the uncertainty of not knowing what's ahead. When they know what to expect, they don't have to worry about yet another new change.

Routines allow for spontaneity.
Yes, routine means you can be more spontaneous! Ironic, but when you base your everyday, normal life on a predictable structure, you're better able to accommodate spontaneity, from weekend fun to a family vacation. With routines, you've built a strong foundation of what to expect so that your kids are more likely to "be game" for new adventures.

Having implemented a solid routine, you'll have an easier time pulling off those out-of-the-ordinary events, from outings to the beach to a large family reunion. Your child will also better adjust to new and potentially scary experiences, such as a trip to the dentist or adjusting to a new school or caregiver.

With the predictability of routine, your child has grown accustomed to a reassuring schedule instead of needing to focus his energy on preparing himself for the new and unexpected— so much so that when the time calls for flexibility, the new experiences will come as a pleasant surprise rather than yet another change to build defenses against.

How to Incorporate Routine

Now that you know the importance of routine, how can you best implement them in your day-to-day life? What are some ways to incorporate routine so you have structure *and* flexibility?

Schedule your basics.

Start with the basics and stick to the same times to do them, such as when your kids:

- Wake up
- Eat breakfast, lunch, dinner, and snacks
- Take a bath
- Take a nap
- Sleep at night

Then for each one, implement the same routine. For instance, during bath time, our twin toddlers are first to go. They remove their clothes, place them in the hamper, and return to the bathroom. I then brush their teeth and run the bath. Once they're in the tub, I wash their hair first then soap their bodies. We dry up, put on their pajamas, read four books, and head to their beds.

That's their bath and bedtime routine every day. We've done this so often, they know what to do each time. They don't protest with each transition, and I don't need to nag to get something done. All I have to say is "bath time," and they scamper off to the bathroom.

Plan activities around your basics.

Now that you've got your basics, plan activities around them. My toddlers take a nap in the middle of the day, so on the weekends, we'll do something before and after naptime. We might do simple errands like going to the farmers' market or attend special events like visiting the beach. With your basics in place, your activities can vary so long as you work around them.

Daily activities on the weekdays will likely be even more regular and routine. For instance, mornings could be walking to the park, with special activities like story time on Wednesdays.

Create traditions.

Traditions establish "big routines" whether grand yearly traditions like holidays or smaller ones like Friday night pizzas. Traditions can also apply to seasons, such as going to the pool in the summers or baking pumpkin pie in the fall.

Traditions can also be simple, like going for a bike ride on Sundays with dad, or sitting out in the yard to drink lemonade on the weekends. My kids know Saturday mornings mean pancakes and strawberries without question.

★

Routines allow you to be consistent but flexible. They give your child the freedom to be curious about his day instead of worrying about potential surprises he has to prepare for. And routines will help you pull off spontaneous events and activities.

You don't need to nag your child—routines do that for you. Imagine all the tasks you'd have to remind him to do if they weren't already part of your routine.

Your children will also be self-sufficient. You won't need to hound him to transition from one task to the next because he does it on his own.

Routines can make the difference between a happy child and an anxious, over-tired one. When your child knows what to expect, he won't have to ask, "What's next?"

Chapter 5

How to Better Communicate with Your Child

Does every interaction with your child feel like a power struggle? You're not able to enjoy her company, especially when all you do is tell her she can't do this or that. She continues to deliberately disobey. She stalls and drags her feet. Everything feels so combative. While you appreciate her strong-willed temperament, you don't like constantly butting heads with her.

These are the times when parenthood feels the most challenging. You've tried asking her nicely to brush her teeth (of course she says "No"). Or you've exuded a stern and strict stance (which only created a clear power struggle).

Don't worry. You can communicate with your child and assert your authority without unnecessary power struggles. You can empathize and involve her in your day-to-day activities without being a pushover. And you can reduce conflict and instead use the struggles as teachable moments.

Before we get into the "how," let's go over the theme we've been talking about in this book: discipline as teaching. Rather than a battle zone between two combative sides, think of it as a classroom between teacher and student. What are we teaching when we're too permissive or when we abuse our power?

> "FOCUS ON CURATING YOUR WORDS TO BETTER COMMUNICATE YOUR GOALS."

Focus on curating your words to better communicate your goals. Not everything has to be a fight between parent and child. A different way of phrasing or communicating with your child is often more effective than scolding or barking orders.

Let's take a look at how to do just that:

First, ask yourself if your communication can improve. Watch how you talk to your child. Are you already assuming a bossy tone? Would you speak that way to a friend, a coworker, or someone you respect?

Clearly, the dynamic between you and your child versus you and a coworker will differ. But regardless, both people deserve respect. You wouldn't think of demanding something of your friend the same way you might of your child. If you don't need to assume a low, firm, or strict voice with her, then don't.

How do you speak to your child when you ask her to do things? Do you do so respectfully, kindly?

Being the authority figure doesn't excuse us from speaking rudely to our kids. Stay calm and composed, even when enforcing rules or when your child talks back. Speak to her as respectfully as you would another adult, or another stranger.

As I mentioned in the chapter on respect, I've been guilty of this many times. When I was frustrated with one of my children and using a harsh tone of voice, my eldest piped up in his brother's defense: "You don't have to say it mean."

Talk about a humbling moment. Since then I've tried to listen to how I sound. Do I sound like a bully? Do I sound mean? When I hear myself sounding mean or negative, I know it's time to pull back and speak kindly.

Not only is speaking disrespectfully not a kind value to model, it's also ineffective. Kids won't listen when they feel disrespected. You're left nagging someone who has tuned out, perpetuating a cycle of not getting anything done.

Focus instead on working together to solve a common problem. Consider yourselves as problem solvers. Your child not wanting to go to bed is just one issue on the surface. When you assume the role of problem solver, you're forced to go deeper. Now the goal is to find ways for her to feel sleepy by bedtime. Maybe you can keep the post-bath time minutes subdued, extending her bedtime by half an hour, or waking her up earlier from her afternoon nap.

Recruit your child to find ways to make that happen. Explain that she's going to bed later so she's sleepier come bedtime. Or that you'll be spending time reading bedtime books instead of having a tickle-fest.

Another common pitfall is *asking* your child to do something that isn't an option. For instance, asking "Do you want to brush your teeth?" or "Should we eat now?" when other options aren't available will set her up for disappointment if she says "no" and her decision isn't honored or enacted. Don't ask when there is no option. Then you end up nagging her to brush her teeth or eat dinner.

Kids need you as part of their team. State the required task as a fact. "Let's go eat—it's dinner time." Or "Here, hold my hand while we cross the street," or even make it fun with "Race you to the bathroom!"

You don't need to exert your authority with every request. Remember that you're working as a team many times. The goal isn't for utmost obedience—sometimes your goal is just to brush her teeth.

Offering Choice as a Way to Empower Children

When given a choice, kids own the task. Putting on a jacket won't seem like Mom's Terrible Idea I Must Rebel Against. Instead, your child gets to decide between a green or gray jacket. Giving choices reduces conflict. I've avoided many tantrums by drawing attention to the choices my kids can make, not the task they're resisting.

Choices empower children. Under the rule of adult decisions nearly all the time, making choices allows your child to voice her opinions. She embraces her choices and is more likely to follow through with them. Adults make most of the decisions in the house, but we also offer our kids choices because we care and respect their decisions.

Offering choices also encourages your child to think for herself. Giving her choices allows her to assert herself and develop critical thinking. She holds herself accountable and decides which option she'd rather do.

While we may not ask our children which new car we should buy, we can still ask them for their opinions. For instance, ask your child whether she'd like to go to the park by your house or the one by school, or if she'd like to eat the banana or the orange.

How can we best offer choices and make sure they're effective?

- **Keep options parent-approved.** Asking if your child wants to sleep now or an hour later isn't realistic if you know she needs to sleep soon.

- **Limit the options.** Offer two options so your child isn't inundated with so many. Aim for two, and if that's not possible, narrow it down ("Pick a book from this shelf").

- **Don't forget you're the adult.** At some point we have to put our foot down when choices aren't heeded. Sometimes kids aren't satisfied with choices, add their own, or ask for them when there *is* no choice. We don't and shouldn't have to succumb to their whims or oblige choices we don't approve.

Label the Action, Not Your Child

Have you been guilty of some of these phrases?

"*You're always giving me trouble.*"

"*I can never take you anywhere.*"

"*Why are you so difficult?*"

I know I have. These phrases negatively label our kids, not the action or behavior. Saying, "You're a bad girl" differs from saying "You did a bad thing." What's the big deal with separating the behavior from your child?

Take a look through the phrases above and you can imagine the effect they might have on your child. Does she *always* give you trouble? Is she truly a difficult child all the time? Attributing misbehavior to her as an innate trait feels discouraging. She'll feel like she's stuck this way without any chance to change.

Your child can change her behavior and actions, but not supposedly inherent traits. Addressing her behavior as "bad" means the behavior is something she can change. Tomorrow, she can do better. She can try harder and communicate clearer. She won't always whine or cry or give you trouble.

But if your child is a "bad girl," then she has no room to change. Say you're disappointed that she lied about finger painting the wall. Rather than call her a liar, say, "I'm upset because you lied about painting the wall." She'll know she can change her actions in the future and choose not to lie again. But if you consider her a liar, then, in her eyes, nothing she can do will change her from being one.

Addressing your child's behavior also allows her to feel guilt, a healthy emotion that teaches her right from wrong. Attributing the behavior to her inherent traits leads her to feel shame instead. What's the difference? Guilt is the awareness of having done something wrong that comes from our actions. Shame, according to Psychology Today, is "...a painful feeling about how we appear to others (and to ourselves) and doesn't necessarily depend on our having done anything."

You can hone your child's sense of guilt by labeling her actions. But pointing out supposed character flaws like saying she's a liar or a bad girl breeds feelings of shame. A child shamed into thinking she's troublesome or a liar has a more difficult time changing her actions.

Your child will understand that you love her despite her disobedience. While you don't love her actions, you will love her no matter what, misbehavior and all.

Loving your child through all her behaviors won't lead her to do the worst possible things. Instead, your love reassures her that her inevitable mistakes are no causes for you to withhold your affection. She's safe being who she is—imperfections and everything—because you love her no matter what. Your child will know you disapprove her behavior, *not* herself.

Rather than labeling your child, find ways for her to change her behavior. For instance, say, "You need to stay in bed, not play with toys," which addresses her behavior. Name-calling or making general statements about not being a good sleeper or always misbehaving at nights isn't productive.

Our kids should know they're wonderful in our eyes no matter what they do. Their actions don't define them and can be corrected.

Communicating with a Child Being Difficult

Giving choices curbs potential conflict and empowers children to make sound decisions. But what happens if your child refuses to obey and says no to everything? Say, for instance, she refuses to put dishes away after meal times even after several requests to do so.

The longer I've been a parent, the more I realize the need to carefully phrase my words. If I can say the same message in a more effective, less bossy way, then I try to do just that. For instance, I try the following techniques when I need my children to listen.

Phrase the task like you're asking for help.
It may not seem like it, but kids want to please their parents, including helping us out. When you need your child to do something, phrase the tasks like you need help with it. "I could use your help to get these dishes in the sink for me while I wipe the table."

She'll feel more independent knowing she's helping you, not just obeying orders. By emphasizing teamwork, you're marking her contribution as essential to the family.

Phrase the task as a perk.

How do you refer to homework, finishing dinner, or putting clothes away?

While homework won't bear the same enthusiasm as receiving a new toy, the way we refer to these tasks can affect our children's outlook on them. Treat tasks as tedious, and your child will respond accordingly. But refer to them as matter of fact or even enjoyable, and your child will do them more willingly.

For instance, homework is inevitable, but it doesn't have to be the boring task it's painted as. Instead, treat it for what it is: something that needs to be done. Go the extra mile and make learning fun and exciting, not something to get out of the way. Promote the love of knowledge, not a worksheet to get through.

It's the difference between "You have to do homework now" and "You can start your homework now." When phrased as a privilege, the chores become something they get to do.

Offer an incentive.

Frame the chore as a means to an (awesome) end. "After we place our dishes in the sink, we can finish that puzzle you liked earlier today."

The focus is on the "after" part—the fun part—and less on the means to get there. The chore isn't the power struggle between you and your child, but something you can do to move on with the day.

Describe, don't demand.

Say your child still hasn't picked up the toys from the floor. If you're like me, you've many times asked silly questions like, "Why haven't you picked up your toys yet?" (As if we expect a reasonable answer to that!)

Instead, try describing instead. "Your toys are still on the floor." Nagging and demanding get tiresome. Describing, on the other hand, is easier to stomach and empowers your child to make the right decision.

Explain why.
I've found that explaining the reason behind my requests has prevented many struggles. My kids respond to the "why" of the tasks much better than simply saying, "Because I said so." Give any reason, so long as it's true and understandable.

For instance, they do homework because their brains get a good workout, or because the teacher needs it the next day. They brush their teeth so they're clean and cavity-free.

Sometimes the reason can even be a "reward." I'm not a fan of conventional rewards, but when phrased as a logical consequence or as part of the routine, kids are likely to finish the task. For instance, your child can start eating dinner so the two of you can play her new board game.

Pick your battles.
Have you counted how many times you say "no" to your child? And not just the word "no," but any variation of it. "Please don't jump on the couch," "We don't hit one another," "Not too loud."

If you're like me, it's a *lot*.

And we have to. We're parents. We provide boundaries and show them appropriate ways to behave. We *need* to tell them not to jump on the couch or hit one another.

But can you imagine living under those circumstances? Being a kid can be tough. Keep that in mind when you're on the brink of another power struggle.

Picking your battles is one part of the equation. On the other side is the importance of following through with consequences and holding your ground, a common parenting conundrum.

In the next chapter, we'll talk about the importance of balancing consistency with flexibility.

Chapter 6

Balancing Consistency with Flexibility

Consider this scenario: Your child knows not to throw the tennis ball indoors, yet he does anyway, chucking the ball through the living room. He seems oblivious to the rules you've reinforced from the first day about throwing only soft balls and saving the heavier ones for outdoors. Your patience is draining and you'd rather ignore his ball tosses to save your sanity. On the other hand, you've heard that you should be consistent with the rules and enforce logical consequences.

Remain consistent or pick your battles? You want to hold your ground so your child knows you're serious about the rules and what to expect. And he needs you to stand your ground and not succumb to his tantrums or whining.

With consistency, your child knows what to expect and understands household rules and responsibilities. He lives within defined boundaries, so he doesn't second-guess expectations. He'll feel less anxious knowing you've got it together. He'll respond the same almost every time.

But do you feel like you discipline all day long, policing your child instead of enjoying your time with him? Sometimes we're too strict. We're scared our kids won't take us seriously if we so much as let one thing lapse. We assume stern discipline is needed so they'll listen. Maybe our own parents raised us this way, and we don't know any different.

Some issues aren't worth the stress. You run the risk of non-stop arguing with your child if you're unwilling to let some things slide.

Life doesn't run on a predictable schedule where nothing out of the ordinary happens. Maybe your child is old enough to watch fireworks this year so you'll need to push bedtime later. Or visitors dropped by and he would rather skip his nap to spend more time with them. Maybe he got sick and needs you to stay by his bed longer than you normally do.

Remain consistent but flexible. Don't try to be one or the other, but rather a bit of both.

You decide which techniques to apply to which situations. What works for your child one day may not work the next. Or what worked for one child one day won't work for another in the same setting. Every child and every setting is different; each instance is unique.

Consider your current situation, not what happened in the past, or what your older child has gone through before. In the next section, we'll discuss how to find a balance between consistency and flexibility.

Balancing Consistency with Flexibility: How to Do It

So, how do you best implement this balance?

For one, define what is and isn't negotiable. We can agree on safety and hygienic reasons. You need to buckle car seats and change messy diapers, regardless of your child's protests. Generally though, each scenario presents a personal choice for each family. For instance, there's no way I'll allow my kids to draw on the wall. I want my walls clean, no matter how much my toddler throws a tantrum. But guess what? An old neighbor of mine couldn't care less about her child scribbling on their walls. To each their own.

Once you've established your non-negotiable rules, be firm but flexible. When your every day is humming along (no one is sick, schedules are all lining up), stay consistent. Don't allow your child to eat bags of chocolate when you want to limit sweets. Be firm when you say he needs to take a bath. Develop a consistent routine to establish a precedent and define your boundaries.

Establish responsibilities and follow through with consequences. Being too lenient is unfair to your child and does him a disservice, not providing him the boundaries he needs. Not holding your ground makes him feel anxious of the rules that seem to flip flop. And with no expectations, he doesn't learn how you want him to behave.

Then, when the time calls for flexibility, allow yourself to bend the rules. Explain to your child *why* you're doing so ("We have guests today we don't see too often, and you want to spend time with them rather than take a nap"). Limit the times you bend the rules so your child understands this is a special occasion instead.

We were having breakfast when my son wanted to eat but didn't want to part with his book. "You can put it on the couch," I told him. "You can have it after you're done eating." This, after all, abides by our efforts not to have toys or books on the table while we're eating. "No," he replied. He started getting fussy.

As I considered letting him keep the book, I worried he'd get confused about the rules if we don't allow toys one day and allow it the next. What if he assumes throwing a fit will get him what he wants? Or worse, what if he has now undermined our authority and will defy future rules we try to impose? What if he won't listen to us in the future?

The answer? Yes. He still listens. Do I *really* need to hound him about the rare times he breaks a rule? Probably not.

Our pediatrician reminded us when our then-toddler was entering his defiant, independent age. She said, "Pick your battles. If he's not hurting anyone, just let him be. If it's not necessary, let it go."

> " DON'T THINK OF INTERACTIONS WITH YOUR CHILD AS A BATTLE ZONE. "

When you make room for flexibility, you're not "losing" to your child. Don't think of interactions with your child as a battle zone. We create disconnection when we pit ourselves against our kids. Consider yourself a teacher or a coach, not an enemy.

And don't worry about setting a bad precedent for your child because you bent the rules one time. ("Great, now he's always going to ask me to buy him a toy whenever we go to the store!"). Because you've established consistency, going off the script will likely not ruin your rules and routine.

The goal of flexibility isn't to make your child happy or to placate a tantrum. Being consistent, yet flexible, teaches him to deal with life circumstances. He'll learn to model his actions after your own. As an adult or an older child, he won't be so rigid to the point of stubbornness. Yet he'll also understand the importance of discipline and following rules.

Chapter 6 - Balancing Consistency with Flexibility

And beneath the parenting do's and don'ts, base your decisions on connection. Ask yourself what you want to teach your child about this moment and the sort of relationship you want to develop. Be on his team with *his* best interests in mind.

Chapter 7

It Starts with You: Model the Right Behavior

So far we've talked about how to create a home that lessens outbursts and standoffs with your child. We discussed establishing routines to reduce nagging and anxiety. We determined the importance of connecting with her and redefined discipline as a way of teaching. We also highlighted the balance of consistency with flexibility.

All great advice—except all the best advice isn't going to work if your own behavior doesn't mirror the kind you want your child to follow.

Sure, we're adults, and certain rules don't apply to us. Our bodies don't need 10—12 hours of sleep the way our kids do, so we don't need to abide by the same bedtime. We're also parents, and as such, need to assume authority and responsibilities. And we all have "bad habits" we can improve, no exceptions.

But if you don't model the behavior you'd like your child to adopt, she's less likely to abide by them. Or worse, she'll follow the rules because of fear-based tactics, not because she understands their benefits or trusts your words.

Modeling the behavior we want to see is one of the best ways to teach. Some common examples of modeling good behavior:

- **Share with others.** Eating snacks? Share a few with your child. Mention how you'd love to share with her.

Chapter 7

When playing a game of building blocks, share a few of your pieces with others. She'll see that everyone shares and enjoys doing so.

- **Speak kindly to your child**, even when she talks back. Has your child been talking back and responding rudely? You might find yourself tempted to blurt terrible words right back. Don't. Hold your temper, take a few breaths, walk away. On so many levels, saying hurtful words in return is wrong. You're modeling the behavior you want her to stop. And with both of you upset, you won't likely calm down or find a resolution.

- **Show empathy.** The next time your child acts up, see the issue from her point of view. Then, before you discipline or redirect, acknowledge her feelings and perspective. And finally, model empathy and describe the emotions she might be feeling: "It's hard to stop doing something you enjoy, isn't it? I'd feel pretty sad too." Use empathy and she'll do the same to better understand others around her.

- **Model kindness.** The kindness we want to see in our kids must begin with ourselves. We need to model the values we want them to emulate. Speak kindly to others, whether family and friends or strangers. Respect your child and be kind to her, in actions and in words. Your actions will teach her more than any lecture or lesson could.

- **Apologize to your child.** We're not exempt from mistakes or their consequences. For children to learn how and when to apologize, we need to take that first step and do so ourselves. Forcing your child to say sorry does little to encourage genuine, heartfelt remorse. Instead, she learns best when you apologize for your mistakes.

Modeling good behavior applies to everything you want your child to do or how you want her to behave.

Maybe you want your child to clean up her toys instead of leaving them on the floor for you to deal with. Or you want her to read every day, eager and without a grumble. Or you'd like to teach the value of gratitude and appreciation instead of the desire for more material goods and the latest fads.

Each of those values and goals are worthy to strive for. But in encouraging your child to pursue those values, you also need to practice them yourself. Don't leave your things all over the house—put them away instead. Read every day for pleasure in front of her. And don't grumble about how little you have or buy the latest and most expensive brands.

Kids model our actions. Actions that conflict with your words confuse your child and create internal conflict. She's not sure which path to follow, or worse, she'll model your behavior despite your admonitions or advice. Your actions don't match your family values, and the rules feel unfair.

No one is perfect, of course. We'll lose our temper, we'll say a bad word, we'll feel lazy about keeping our home clean. Even after reading this book, I guarantee you and I will both make mistakes. And that's okay—we make and hopefully learn from them. Modeling the behavior you want your child to exemplify doesn't mean being perfect.

Instead, when mistakes happen—and they will—use them as an opportunity to model good behavior. Apologize so she can see how to do so gracefully and kindly. Admit the areas you can improve or make a goal to not repeat them again. We're not out to be perfect models. But we can still hold ourselves accountable to the same expectations we've set for our children.

Excusing yourself from the same standards wastes your time. Spewing parenting advice without modeling them is an inefficient way to discipline.

Focus on the values you want her to uphold, including behavior. The best way to do so is to *be* the kind of adult you'd want her to grow up to be.

Thus far, we've discussed preventative measures and how to decrease the chances of conflict with our children. From giving your child your full attention to modeling good behavior, these steps lessen the likelihood of an outburst or standoff from occurring in the first place.

But as we all know, even *some* conflict is inevitable and normal. No amount of parenting hacks can (nor should) prevent them from happening at all.

In the next section, we'll talk about how to handle conflict when it does happen. You'll learn how to best communicate with your child when she's upset (it's not through lectures, I'll tell you that!). We'll talk about the lessons you want her to learn from her outburst. We'll discuss the importance of parenting calmly and how to do just that.

PART TWO

HOW TO HANDLE
YOUR CHILD'S MISBEHAVIOR

Chapter 8

Discipline: The *Real* Definition

You've tried common discipline techniques such as time-outs to get your child to behave. And they seem to work in the short-term. Your child has stopped misbehaving and has given you peace and quiet, even if only for a few minutes.

But what has he learned about regulating his emotions, or interacting with others? Will he base his decisions on fear of punishment or to avoid angering you? Will he know how to better communicate with words? And will he act with genuine introspection the next time, or will he obey simply to avoid a time-out?

It's no surprise that no matter how many times you've disciplined, the same behaviors keep happening. You're stuck in the same cycle without seeing long-term change. And maybe you've assumed the methods you've tried were the only way to go.

> " YOUR BIGGER GOAL IS TO GIVE YOUR CHILD THE SKILLS TO BETTER COPE WITH HIS EMOTIONS IN THE FIRST PLACE. "

Your intentions are in the right place—we all want kids who behave. You just need a new approach to discipline. You've realized your goal isn't only to stop the behavior as it's happening.

Your bigger goal is to give your child the skills to better cope with his emotions in the first place.

What do you think of when you hear the word "discipline"?

Maybe you thought about time-outs, distraction, or redirection. Perhaps you thought about the consequences you need to give and the best ways to follow through with them. Maybe you think of discipline as the exhausting part of parenting—the draining episodes and power struggles with your child.

But like we discussed in previous chapters, discipline is nothing more than this: teaching and helping your child to behave.

It's a new way of thinking about discipline, isn't it? Discipline isn't just punishment, consequences, or what to do when kids misbehave. Discipline is teaching our kids how to act.

Discipline is what parents do when children don't behave properly or safely. It's when we teach them to regulate their emotions during a tantrum. When we provide boundaries wide enough for our children to explore but confined enough so they feel safe.

You help your child overcome the anxieties and emotions that led him to misbehave. And you guide him toward the best ways to express himself and behave well.

And here's the best part: discipline doesn't have to be the draining, no-end-in-sight fiasco you've dreaded in the past. You won't have the parent-child standoff or the typical "Because I said so!" yelling match.

Sure, tantrums and outbursts are never pleasant—you won't ever look forward to them or find them enjoyable. But when you learn to discipline effectively, you won't lose your temper so much. You'll be intentional with your actions, knowing each one has a purpose and an end goal. You'll connect with your child's needs and give him the skills to cope and deal with his emotions in the future.

One of the best ways to start is to ask yourself one simple question before disciplining your child. One question to change your mindset before reacting. A simple question, but one packed with many answers: "Why?"

Let's say your toddler hit his brother in the face, for no apparent reason. Or he threw food all over the table. Or he won't stop fussing or crying, regardless of your many attempts to soothe him.

Next thing you know, you've lost your temper. You've asked him to say "sorry" or forced him to share a toy they were fighting over. You tried a time-out, to no avail.

But rather than the teachable moment you were hoping for, your child is even more miserable.

The solution? Ask yourself "Why?" The process of asking as well as the answers you'll get will reveal a lot.

Get the whole story.
First, you're forced to consider your child's point of view. Why did your child hit his brother in the face, for what seemed like no reason (Here's a tip: there's *always* a reason)? Was he jealous that he had gotten a favorite toy first? Had he been harboring a grudge and reached a breaking point? Was his brother unintentionally inching over too much and invading his space?

Ask yourself why your child is behaving the way he is and you'll see the predicament in a new light. Your child's behavior didn't happen because he just wanted to hit his brother. Underlying reasons led him to do it.

Ask yourself why your child is acting the way he does. Simple as that. You're forced to discover the reasons behind his confusing or frustrating behavior. Sometimes you'll come up with a simple answer like, "He must be hungry," or "Oh, he skipped his nap today."

Other times, the reasons aren't obvious and you'll need to consider his point of view. For example, one time, my twins had been fighting over a prized toy. One got to play with the toy while the other had to wait his turn. Later, when he finished playing, I had him tell his brother he could now use the toy. He obliged and told his brother, who had been playing trains in the next room, that he could play with the toy now. But rather than run to the coveted toy, his twin brother reacted by hitting him.

Immediately, I disciplined the offending boy: "We do not hit. Your brother was telling you he finished with the toy and that you can play with it." I didn't understand how he could go from playing with trains to hitting his brother.

Only later did I realize why: he was still upset. Playing with trains didn't mean he was over it. He had been playing with trains as a way to self-soothe from an earlier argument over the special toy. He was still harboring resentment towards his brother.

Asking myself "why" would have helped me be more empathetic towards both of them. I wouldn't have immediately sided with the "victim."

Asking "why" also encourages you to show empathy. When you ask *why* your child acts up, you'll often find a reason that you can empathize with. Let's say you're about to get angry with your child for dropping her plate on the way to the sink. With empathy, you realize she made a mess because she was only trying to be helpful.

Disciplining children isn't always necessary when you understand why they act the way they do. The next time your child acts difficult, confusing, or annoying, ask "why." Listen to what your child says, and what your gut tells you. You may find that the reason itself is much deeper or even simpler than you first assumed.

What's your goal?
Second, asking yourself why you're disciplining will make you think about *your* end goal. Sure, your end goal might be to stop the behavior or to reinforce your authority. Maybe you'll realize you don't even have a reason to discipline.

When you ask yourself why you're disciplining, the answer is what you want your child to learn. "Discipline" is teaching. As your child's primary teacher, what would you like him to learn from this moment? Maybe you want him to learn how to communicate better and use words instead of whining. Or you want him to take turns with other kids at the park and learn the value of sharing and playing with others. Maybe you'd like him to learn how to wait and deal with boredom.

I know it's not the easiest thing to do. Every piece of advice I mention in this book is advice I've had to give myself. Dealing with an angry child in the middle of a tantrum and turning it into a teachable moment is *tough*. I've lost my temper and yelled at my kids many times. Even those times when I've been able to remain calm haven't always been pleasant. I felt fake trying to show my love and affection while feeling irritable inside.

It's hard. But the whole point of discipline—the whole point of parenting, really—is what you want to your child to learn. Then focus on helping your child reach those goals. Think about the values and skills you'd like him to develop as he grows into adulthood.

Respond, don't react.

Asking "why" also helps you pause. You parent mindfully when you take a breath and remove yourself from the incident. You're more likely to assess the problem from all angles instead of resorting to anger or frustration.

That quick pause leads you to respond, not react. Maybe you realize you don't even have to discipline or get angry and that you had made false assumptions. Or you're better able to redirect your child towards something more appropriate. Your thought process can go something like, "Why did he just dump that box of cereal on the floor? (Pause.) Maybe he was curious, not being mischievous. Let me give him a box of Lego to play with instead."

Again, this is tough stuff. Some days are easier, like when you give yourself a mental prep and are on your A-game for the day. Other times, you're tired—dealing with another disciplining moment is exhausting and the last thing you want to do.

To parent with purpose, let go of the old notion of discipline as punishment for your child. Or that discipline is thinking of something bad enough so your child will "learn his lesson." Or that discipline is merely time-out or consequences.

Discipline teaches your child skills, from communicating with others to behaving well in public. The end goal is to raise a future adult. A confident, kind child who can get along well with others. A future adult who can regulate himself through different scenarios. A person who will do all that without needing someone to coerce him into it.

Only in discovering *why* your child is acting that way will you be able to teach him how to improve and learn.

The answers to your "why" can be simple, from hunger to tiredness. And sometimes the answers can run deeper like feeling anxious about changes at home.

Then ask yourself what you want your child to get out of this. What lesson do you want to teach your child? Understand his frame of mind and you'll be more patient and effective with your child. You can turn a potential power struggle into a positive, relationship-building moment.

In the next chapter, we'll bust the common myths of time-outs, and learn why time-ins are much more effective.

Chapter 9

Why You Need to Connect with Your Child Even through the Worst

Getting frustrated with our kids is easy, isn't it? Everyone is ready to head out the door but one of them sulks and refuses to leave. Or you took the family to the beach hoping to have fun but your toddler cried the entire time. How about when you catch your child jumping on the couch when you've already told her many times not to do that?

You don't want a relationship filled with conflict and fighting. Or to face those tween or teenage years dealing with the same issues, magnified times ten. And you want to actually enjoy your time with your child, not spend your days refereeing or policing her all day long.

And so you may feel tempted to banish your child to time-out, sending her to her room to cry and leave everyone else in peace. Maybe you've also threatened punishments, hoping to stop the outburst right then and there. You may have even lost your temper and yelled, then felt guilty for having done so.

These acts of defiance, tantrums, and meltdowns can challenge even the calmest of parents. We've all gone through these, tried the same methods, and gotten the same dismal results.

The good news is you *can* have a loving relationship, raise well-behaved children, and discipline calmly and proactively.

These moments, the most challenging ones, are the times we need to draw our kids in even closer. Forget time-outs, or building up a wall, or being so stern and rigid to the point of having power struggles.

Drawing our kids closer during outbursts seems counterintuitive, especially when we're supposed to reinforce and praise positive behavior. Paying attention to our kids when they're behaving well seems reasonable. Wouldn't that mean that we ignore them when they're misbehaving?

Not at all. Sending your child to her room will make her feel like you only want her around when she's happy and cheerful, not when she's upset and angry. She might assume you withhold your affection when she misbehaves. And that she needs to determine what she did wrong, all by herself.

We can't judge their emotions, hugging and kissing them when they're happy but withholding affection when they're angry. Our kids will think, "Mom kisses me when I feel happy or excited, but then yells or ignores me when I feel sad, angry, or scared." We need to love and support our kids through *all* emotions—happy or sad, silly or angry.

It boils down to this: The times we least feel like loving our kids are when they need us the most.

Are you then enabling misbehavior? No. Enabling misbehavior is letting your child continue to misbehave. She has to abide by your 30-minutes-of-television-a-day rule, tantrum or not. She still needs boundaries and can't continue to climb the bookshelves. You won't encourage her to have more tantrums by holding her close as she cries into your arms. You're not promoting misbehavior because you sat nearby and rubbed her back rather than putting her in time-out.

In fact, these unconditional acts of love calm your child faster and avoid putting her on the defense. You both know there's a problem, and you're both committed to helping her get through it. You let her know you understand what she's going through. You've got her back, both at her best *and* worst moments.

And perhaps the most important reason we need to connect with our kids when they're out of sorts? They're scared. It doesn't feel good to *them* to throw a tantrum or yell at their parents. They're not secretly giddy as they yell and scream or ignore you. Tantrums in themselves are scary enough. Now imagine feeling like no one—not even your parents—can put a stop to them.

Instead of time-out and punishment, use these moments to draw your child in. To the inconsolable child in the middle of an outburst, stay nearby and hold her if he lets you. Without saying a word, send the message that you're here for her when she's ready to be consoled. To the child overwhelmed with her emotions, holding her in your arms can break through her defensiveness. She knows she's still loved and safe with you.

And I get it—connecting with your child doesn't mean you'll always enjoy it. Trying to coerce a defiant child to do something is exhausting. I can't tell you how many times I've looked at the clock wondering how long this episode will last. Tantrums suck, big time.

But we're hoping for long-term goals. Sending your child to time-out or yelling will give you "instant results," but through fear-based parenting. Connecting with her instead builds a long-lasting foundation for your relationship. And you'll teach her skills to prevent and lessen future outbursts.

Now that you know the importance of connecting with your child, let's look at different ways to do so.

How to Connect with Your Child

Use and teach empathy.

How easy it is to see only the surface of misbehavior. Imagine, for instance, a child who refuses to get in the car to leave. All you see is a defiant child not listening or doing what she's told. "She should know better," you might think. You're preoccupied with how late you're running or the big deal she makes out of every little thing.

Empathy, however, forces you to put yourself in your child's shoes. Asking "why" makes you think of reasons she's acting up. You're then able to guess that she got her feelings hurt when she fought with her brother, or that she's scared of taking gymnastic lessons, for example.

Acknowledge what it must feel like from your child's perspective. One day, my son and I were walking from school to the car when he realized he lost the happy face sticker his teacher placed on his hand.

"I want to go back and look for it," he whimpered with his chin quivering. Meanwhile, I wanted to get to the car as fast as possible and avoid a public outburst. I needed to get home in time to send the nanny home and cook dinner. The quickest way would've been to drag my crying son and strap him into the seat. But I realized empathizing with his emotions would likely be more effective.

"You lost the sticker on your hand? You feel pretty bad you don't have it anymore, don't you?" I said. "You felt special when Ms. M gave that to you, and now you feel sad you don't have it anymore. I'd feel pretty sad too if I lost something special. Tell you what: is there another sticker at home we can put on your hand? Maybe you can show Ms. M your new sticker tomorrow."

That incident smoothed over much quicker than if I had told him to get over it. Or that the sticker wasn't important (even if to me, *it's just a darn sticker*). I may have spent more time at the school than I would've wanted ("We need to get home by 4!" I kept thinking). But my heart felt lighter than it would have if I had simply dismissed his emotions and dragged him home.

When you practice empathy, you can see why your child is acting the way she is. She feels like she has an ally in you when you relate to her feelings. Teaching your child empathy helps her interact with others, including you. She knows we all have similar feelings and predicaments and how to use words and feelings to communicate.

It's so easy to say "It's okay" and dismiss your child's emotions. You may have done so to soothe her after she has fallen and gotten hurt. Or maybe you've tried to rid her of unpleasant feelings like fear, uncertainty, or the confusion that ensues after a fight with a friend.

But these emotions are real to your child—as real as your own emotions. She may not be ready to dismiss her feelings right away. She feels a wide range of emotions—anxiety, fear, jealousy—but has limited understanding and language to express them. Acknowledging her emotions does the following:

- **Provides a chance to sort through feelings.** Imagine you got in a fight with a friend and feel jealous, rejected, or anxious. So you turn to your mom for support, except she says, "It's okay, you'll get over it." It's *not* okay to you, at least not yet. Dismissing your child's emotions can feel the same for her. Even if you know she'll be okay, she still needs that time to simply vent and have the space to own her feelings.

- **Makes your child feel respected.** Acknowledging your child's emotions respects her feelings—they're no less valid than the feelings of an adult. She won't feel belittled for being afraid of shadows or upset when another kid took her shovel. When you address her fears instead of chiding her with, "Are you being a scaredy-cat?" she'll know you take her emotions seriously.

- **Offers a quicker way to work through unpleasant emotions.** You help your child resolve uncertain feelings she may have rather than burying it for later. When my son used to cry at bath time, I learned to work around his fears rather than force him to bathe or dismiss his emotions. I set the faucet to a slow trickle instead of a steady downpour. I raised the temperature. I used my hands instead of a washcloth. He became more comfortable with bath time and stopped crying.

In addition to expressing empathy, teach your child how to use it as well. Get in the habit of discussion emotions, even those of others. Let's say your kids got in a fight. Acknowledge both their feelings, "Look at your sister crying. She got hurt when you pushed her. It doesn't feel good to have someone push us." Then to your daughter you might say, "He didn't like it when you knocked down his blocks. He was working hard on building that bridge and now he has to start over."

Encourage your child to put herself in another person's shoes and imagine being on the receiving end of others' actions. When you read books, discuss the characters' feelings. "Why do you think the dog felt sad when the other classmates wouldn't believe his story?" You can also discuss your own feelings. "I get hurt when you talk back to me that way," or "I'm so excited to spend the day with you!"

Honor the impulse.

I found this wonderful phrase, "honor the impulse," from the book *Becoming the Parent You Want to Be* by Laura Davis and Janis Keyser. Honoring your child's impulse identifies and acknowledges the reason why your child acted the way she did. You'll realize her actions didn't stem from just being mischievous.

Let's say your child colored the walls with crayon. Pretty difficult to stomach, right? You wonder what in the world she was thinking. You assume she should've known better. And you're ready to react with a stern voice and enough punishments to drive the point across.

But don't start disciplining, raising your voice, or using this as a "teachable moment" just yet. Instead, step back and acknowledge the impulses or motives that drove her to color on the walls.

You might see that your child only wanted to color. Curiosity drove her to wonder why rubbing a colored stick against the wall would add marks. Maybe she decided to test the results with the other sticks and see what would happen.

The wall isn't the place to explore her coloring curiosity. Later, you'll explain to her that you don't color on walls, but rather on paper. But for now, it's important to understand that her intention wasn't to disobey or get you angry. Even if the actions were inappropriate, her impulse was simply to color. Coloring is awesome—a skill you'd want her to have—but she needs to learn the places she can and can't do so.

Honoring your child's impulse says you're on her side. You empathize with her motives, regardless of her behavior. You acknowledge that the impulse—coloring—is encouraged, but she just needs to do so in an appropriate way.

Allow your child to cry.

Ever heard people say "Stop crying" to a child? We're uncomfortable with tears. We assume our job is to comfort our child as fast as possible. A five-minute tantrum is a success, while an hour-long cry-fest signals failure.

But crying can be a good thing. Your role as a parent isn't to prevent your child from crying or to try to cheer her up as soon as possible—and it's definitely not to tell her to stop crying.

Let your child cry. Crying is cathartic and allows her to release pent up emotions bound to come out anyway. Hushing her up will only make the next episode worse.

What should you do instead of telling your child to stop crying? Let her cry with you by her side. Hold her, rock her side to side, and whisper a few comforting phrases like, "I know," "It hurts, doesn't it?" or "You feel sad." That's all. No need to make her stop crying sooner than later.

Imagine yourself in her shoes. Say you had a *terrible* day: you fought with your best friend. You're so upset, sad, and anxious. You're crying your eyes out, and your spouse says, "Stop crying."

It doesn't feel good, does it?

Not only does allowing your child to cry with you respect her feelings, it's also a faster way to actually help your child stop crying. Telling her to stop crying raises her defenses, isolates her away from you, and will only make her cry even longer. But allowing her to cry soothes her and will stop the crying sooner.

Let your child cry with you. You're not enabling poor behavior or raising someone who will cry all the time. We *all* need to release frustration through tears sometimes.

Laugh with your child.

Another tactic if your child is crying or whining is to use laughter. Laughing releases the same bottled-up frustrations as crying. If she acts combative, whines, or behaves otherwise unpleasant, see if you can make her laugh.

On one memorable occasion, my two-year-old was whining, asking me to play cars. Except I could tell he was asking just to ask. Even if I did play cars, he'd find something else to whine about. He wasn't on the verge of crying just yet, so I tried to make him laugh instead.

I picked him up and blew raspberries on his belly. He resisted at first, but his whining soon turned to full-blown laughter. Any time he tried to whine again, I made him laugh. After five minutes of this, he decided he could, after all, play cars by himself just fine.

This isn't to say you should make your child laugh every time she's on the verge of crying. Take it case by case.

Nor does this mean we turn to laughter as a distraction. If your child feels truly upset or is in no mood to laugh, don't bother trying to make her laugh. Try listening or holding her close instead. But many times, laughter deflects misbehavior and is all your child needs to release frustration and pent-up energy.

Rather than sending your child off to time-out or get angry with her, choose instead to connect. Without a word, you send the message that you're there for her even (and especially) when she's acting up. You've got her back even when she's unpleasant to be with. You're not going to send her off when she's upset and only hang out with her when she feels happy.

So you stay nearby, easing her frustration and anxiety with a warm embrace. You don't say much, just a simple, "It hurts, doesn't it?" or "I know, I know." You let her cry to you as you would want to cry to a friend when you're feeling upset or down.

Then once she's calm, use empathy. Ask yourself what she must be going through, and teach her how to use empathy with others. Acknowledge her emotions so she knows what these strange and heavy feelings are. She'll understand everyone goes through them, even you. That feelings come and will eventually go.

Honor the impulse as well. Acknowledge the reason your child acted the way she did. You'll see that it probably wasn't to get you upset. She may have even been trying to help, or was curious, or simply didn't know any better. Rather than sending her off by herself, help her find ways to cope with her emotions.

Your child will begin initiating these methods herself. She'll use empathy and learn to take turns with others. She'll say she's hungry rather than whine. She'll rely less and less on you to guide her through her outbursts as she learns to do them on her own.

Now that you've connected with your child as your first step in discipline, the next is to redirect her towards appropriate ways to behave.

Chapter 10

Redirection: Teaching Your Child the Appropriate Ways to Behave

You caught your child coloring on the wall, jumping on the couch or about to throw the remote control across the room. You've connected and understood the real definition of discipline. You've calmed down from the initial shock of seeing your crayon-colored walls. Now it's time to address his behavior. But first, let's talk about the difference between two common approaches: redirection or distraction.

Parents use both methods to discipline and prevent outbursts. With similar intentions, redirection and distraction are sometimes confused with one another, or used interchangeably. But as you'll see, the two differ, and you'll learn why I prefer one over the other.

Let's go back to one of the scenarios I painted earlier: You walk into your living room and see your child about to throw the remote control across the room.

You could use distraction to divert him to something new and convince him not to throw the remote control: "Look at your new blocks—let's play with those instead." You have achieved your goal of preventing your child from throwing the remote control.

With *redirection*, you also prevent him from throwing the remote control but with the added benefit of assessing his motives first: he wanted to throw. Throwing isn't terrible. You'd *want* your child to develop this skill and you'd certainly encourage him to do so in another setting.

And so you redirect. You find something similar while still honoring the impulse. "Looks like you want to throw the remote control. We don't throw the remote control because you might break things. You can throw this soft ball instead."

See the difference?

Both methods stop the behavior. But redirection is more effective since it teaches your child why that particular behavior is inappropriate. With distraction, sure he'll figure out that you can throw balls but not remote controls. But redirection clearly explains why.

The Benefits of Redirection

- Redirection honors your child's impulses. Distracting him with blocks dismisses his initial desire to throw. Redirection on the other hand acknowledges his impulses and curiosity and steers him to an appropriate activity that allows him to do so. Say he's about to color on your books. Acknowledge his desire to color rather than ignoring it with another random activity ("Play with your truck instead").

- Redirection reassures your child that his intentions aren't wrong and he's not in trouble. We can agree coloring is awesome! But we do need to define the times it's acceptable (in a coloring book) and when it's not (in mommy's books). With redirection, he knows you're on his side to help him find an alternative.

- And finally, redirection also applies to the way your child communicates with you. If he says something rude or talks back, offer a different way to convey the same message while honoring his emotions.

Distraction doesn't leave much room to explain the rules. If averting a meltdown means finding a distraction, we don't teach why the initial behavior was wrong. Your child should know why it's not okay to climb on the bookshelf or to throw the remote control.

Your child is entitled to his feelings, even unpleasant ones like disappointment, anger, or frustration. However, he can't express those emotions in mean ways. Honor the impulse by empathizing with his feelings, but show him another way to say it.

"Looks like you're mad because you want to keep playing your game," you might begin. "But we don't talk that way to one another. Say, 'Just a minute,' in a kinder tone next time."

Let's take a look at another example: your kids are fighting over a toy. You could distract one or both of them with a different toy and hope they'll forget about the original one. Doing so will probably avert a meltdown or fight. But your kids won't get to learn about turn-taking or how to solve social conflicts.

This happens often with my own kids. For instance, my twins could be fighting over the same teddy bear. I could easily distract one or both of them with another toy, but I try to challenge them to take turns instead. Since we've done this many times, they're learning more and more to play together and take turns on their own (mostly!).

Distraction is more of a way to placate our kids at any cost. We do whatever it takes to avoid a meltdown or be the "bad guy." Sure, you may have averted a meltdown or kept your books from getting colored even more, but you would've missed out on several opportunities to honor your child's impulse, explain the rules, or encourage conflict resolution.

Now you know the difference between redirection and distraction and why I prefer one over the other. Next, let's put it into action:

1. **Honor the impulse.** Before you discipline, determine your child's intentions.

2. **Explain why.** Your child's impulses may be appropriate, but he still needs to learn why that particular action isn't allowed.

3. **Redirect to an appropriate activity that honors the impulse.** Offer a similar yet appropriate activity that hones your child's impulse. Similarly, encourage conflict resolution if your kids are fighting with one another.

Honor the impulse.

As we discussed in the previous chapter, honoring the impulse acknowledges your child's motives and forces you to peel away assumptions you may have had. Find your child's underlying intentions. You'll start to see that his motive probably wasn't to get you upset or doing something he wasn't supposed to.

Give a reason.

Have you blurted the phrase, "Because I said so!"? You're not the only one. It's easy to say, especially with your child's constant questions of "why?" I've run out of patience having to explain why we have to eat dinner now or put away the toys.

But kids respond well to reasons why they can or can't do something. Your child is more likely to cooperate and get into the car seat when you explain that they keep him safe, for instance.

Given a reason, your child feels like you're not just being "the mean guy" and bossing him around. Speaking to his level, you explain why he must now put away his toys, or head home from the park, or not stand on the coffee table.

You also explain the reason to teach him your family rules, from treating others nicely so they don't get hurt to not running with pencils so he don't poke himself in the eye.

Redirect to a more appropriate behavior.

You've understood what caused your child to misbehave (he wanted to color). And you've told him the reasons and rules (the walls are hard to clean and not the right place to color). Now, redirect to a similar and appropriate way to honor his impulse to color (handing him sheets of paper).

Maybe your child wants to throw the remote control (honor the impulse). Explain that doing so can break things or hurt other people (give the reason). Tell him to throw the soft ball or stuffed animal instead (redirect).

Redirect your child to similar activities that still respects his play and learning. Otherwise, he won't know what to make of the new red ball you handed him when all he wanted to do was climb the bookshelf.

Some days, redirecting will be the *last* thing we'll think about (such as when your child is about to grab scissors or run toward the street). We react too hastily. We can't think fast enough. Sometimes an alternative just isn't feasible.

But if possible, find the reason your child behaved the way he did. Teach him why his actions were wrong, then show him a more appropriate alternative. Redirect instead of distract, punish, or scold.

Continue to do this and you will help your child feel less confused about the rules. ("Why did mom get upset when I jumped on the couch, since she was so excited about me jumping at the park?")

He'll learn not to repeat misbehavior when you've explained why. And you'll avoid conflict when you understand his intention wasn't wrong.

Like I mentioned, we can redirect in most cases. But what about the times when even *that* doesn't work? Your child refuses to throw the soft ball, or color on paper, or jump on the floor instead of the couch. Maybe he even continues to speak rudely or fight with his siblings despite your effort to honor the impulse or redirect his actions elsewhere.

In the next chapter, we'll talk about what to do when your child refuses to comply and continues to misbehave. You'll learn the importance of following through with consequences and effective ways to do so.

Chapter 11

Following through with Consequences

"If you aren't able to play with the golf clubs correctly," I told my toddler, "I'll have to put them away until you're ready to use them." As you might expect from a two-year-old, he continued to swing the clubs in the air. I knew taking them away would mean instant tears, but I was afraid he would hit his brothers in the face. No parent wants to see her child cry, but following through with consequences was more important than avoiding a tantrum.

Still, that doesn't make enforcing the rules any easier. We don't like seeing our kids upset. Following through with consequences can feel really, *really* draining. Caving in and letting the behavior slip may seem much easier, especially when our kids act remorseful.

Maybe you tried putting your foot down in the past, threatening your child with consequences. It worked a few times, but now she caught on. Or perhaps you see her disappointment and give her another chance. And another, and another.

You've empathized with your child ("I know you're really excited about those new golf clubs"). You've shown her the correct way to play with her toys ("Swing it gently and low to the ground, not above your head"). You've even tried redirecting her to a similar activity—except she's still not listening.

Now you need to follow through with consequences and choose the *logical* ones to enforce. Not just any consequence will do.

Before we get into how to do just that, let's talk about a common struggle among many parents: standing your ground in the first place.

Your Child Needs Boundaries

Bending to your child's requests seems easier than subjecting yourself to yet another meltdown. You have too many things on your plate to say "no" to her. Maybe you even assume your job as a parent is to make her happy and meet her needs and wants as much as possible.

Except to a child, getting your way every single time doesn't feel good. Ironic but true: despite her protests to have it her way, she actually needs you to stand your ground instead.

Conceding and catering to your child's every tantrum or standoff *doesn't* feel good to her. She's scared her tantrums and emotions are stronger than you can handle. She feels like no one can protect her from her unpleasant emotions.

Tantrums in themselves are overwhelming enough for your child to experience. Now imagine feeling like no one—not even your parents—can put a stop to them.

Having so much power terrifies kids. They don't want free reign to make choices beyond the few that they can handle. Yes, you should encourage your child to explore and assert herself... but only within the boundaries you establish.

Interestingly, setting limits and following through reassures your child that you care. Despite her protests, she wants boundaries. She *wants* someone to care enough to go through the hassles of enforcing limits.

We need to be the folks who can stand up to the tantrums, help our kids get through them, and follow through with our word. Firmly, but kindly, and with our child's best intentions.

The Benefits of Following through with Consequences

Your child will respect your authority.

"If you keep throwing those toys, we're leaving the library," I once heard a woman tell her grandson. The boy was full of energy and disrupting other children.

Unfortunately, he didn't stop throwing the toys. Even more unfortunate, the grandmother continued to stay and allow her grandchild to disrupt others around him.

Something told me the boy's disregard and the grandmother's leniency weren't new to their relationship. We discussed the importance of flexibility in an earlier chapter, and how you don't want to be too rigid or stubborn about "losing" to your child. *Consistency with flexibility.*

But your child will call your bluff when you don't hold her accountable or if you dismiss the rules repeatedly. Your consequences become empty threats, just another phrase that won't bear any action.

No one wants to leave a family gathering because your toddler is overtired and throwing a tantrum. You don't feel any better when you cut reading time short because your child continues to misbehave. But following through establishes limits for both of you. You know when enough is enough.

Similarly, following through with consequences reinforces the trust your child places on you. While you may not win short-term favor, in the long run, you're gaining her trust when you continually stick to your word. The less fickle and the more consistent you implement your rules, the more she'll trust you.

Your child will learn right from wrong.

Remember when we discussed discipline as teaching? You also teach your child the natural and logical consequences of her behavior. Misbehaving and not taking care of a toy means she's not ready to play with it right now. Talking back isn't the way to express frustration; it needs to be better communicated.

If you don't enforce consequences, your child learns that her behaviors have no limits. She'll grow up with the false assumption that the world bends to her whims.

Your child *won't* thrive in total freedom. Nor has she reached an age to make mature decisions on her own. She needs someone to teach her right from wrong and have her best intentions in mind.

Your child will learn accountability.

No finger-pointing here. Kids learn accountability for decisions they make when the consequences tie directly with their choices. *They* didn't pick up the toys = *They* don't get to play with them. Parents are enforcers, but a child's actions determined the outcome.

Kids will think through and deliberate their choices more knowing they carry consequences. Following through with consequences keeps them from making impulsive decisions.

Keep in mind, however, that we can't hold kids accountable for everything. If your child lost her sweater, you can't expect her to go cold the rest of winter, regardless of how careless she may have been in leaving it behind at the park.

Think smaller infractions like maintaining a prized toy or not changing her order to orange juice right when she receives her lemonade.

We've learned the benefits of following through with consequences: your child learns from and thrives within boundaries. She'll respect your authority instead of calling your bluff. She'll learn right from wrong, and she's held accountable for the decisions she makes.

Now that you know the benefits, how can you best follow through with consequences?

How to Follow through with Consequences

Be calm and communicate without anger or lecturing.

We'll talk more about the benefits of parenting calmly in later chapters. For now, do your best to parent without anger (easier said than done, I know). State the consequences as matter-of-fact, and follow through just as calmly. By speaking calmly, you emphasize that the consequences are a result of your child's actions. You're not the "mean mommy" overreacting or scolding because you're in a bad mood. You're simply enforcing the consequences of her behavior. The best part? Her response will likely remain calm as well. No uproar, resentment, or further stubbornness.

I've noticed a huge shift when I remain calm and not angry with following through. My kids feed off of my mood, so the more upset I am, the worse they react. But when I bite the bullet and parent calmly, the less defensive and the more accommodating they become.

Offer *logical* consequences.

Discipline is most effective when logical consequences follow your child's behavior. Taking away her play dough because she continued to sprinkle it all over the floor makes sense. Taking away her fire truck, even if it's her favorite, doesn't.

Is your child thrashing around and breaking a toy? A logical consequence may be to stash the toy away until she learns not to repeat her actions. Telling her she can't go to the park doesn't tie in to the behavior. Another example of this is to take away the markers she's using to draw on herself. Avoid threatening your kids with, "If you don't stop drawing markers all over yourself, I'm going to take away your special bear."

Logical consequences are another reason I'm not a fan of time-outs. Your child receives the same consequence regardless of the action. She isn't going to think about what she did wrong or how she can improve herself. Instead, she's growing resentful feeling like an injustice has been done to her.

Logical consequences teach your child the results of her behavior. She'll have a better understanding next time of what will happen if she misbehaves again.

Offer consequences you'll actually enforce.

Another common mistake is threatening your child with something you know you won't do. I've caught myself saying, "All right, I'm leaving now. See you later!" in an attempt to hurry my kids along out the door. As if I would actually leave without them. Farfetched consequences may work a few times because your child believes you, but not only are these consequences lies, she'll catch on and will likely not believe you the next time.

Stick to feasible consequences. Your child can't play in the morning because she took too long putting on clothes, not that she won't be going to Disneyland with the family.

Her consequence should be a logical result of her behavior.

Remember to use consequences appropriate for your child's age and stage, too. Don't expect her to vacuum the mess she made if she doesn't know how or is too young to do so. Decide on consequences within her abilities.

Remember to be consistent.

Have you gone on a "discipline binge" for two weeks, only to call it off right after? Like we discussed in earlier chapters, consistency is key. Regularly following through with consequences helps your child understand the family boundaries.

We're all human and can't be on our A-game 100% of the time. Life circumstances happen, and we need room for flexibility and special occasions. Sometimes we snap, or we're simply too tired to discipline. It happens to all of us.

But the more consistent you are—however difficult those first few times—the better discipline gets. Your child will start to pay attention. She'll remember that you stick to your word. She'll be less likely to misbehave because she knows what happens when she does.

Our job as parents isn't to make our kids happy. Nor is it to avoid conflict at all costs, caving in and allowing your family rules and values to slip. However difficult enforcing rules and following through with consequences may be, our kids need us to establish boundaries.

> " WHAT LESSONS DO WE TEACH OUR KIDS WHEN
> WE DON'T SET LIMITS? "

Discipline, and parenting, is about teaching. What lessons do we teach our kids when we don't set limits?

Establishing boundaries urges your child to listen and take your word seriously. She'll thrive under predictability and boundaries. While it may be tough to put your foot down, the more consistent you are, the less you'll need to assert your authority. Following through with consequences shows you care about what she can learn from this and teaches her right from wrong.

Your goal isn't to be strict and rigid without taking into account life circumstances. Flexibility is necessary, as we discussed. But resorting to its opposite extreme will lead to even more defiance.

When done with respect, following through with consequences isn't about punishment. It steers your child toward the behaviors you want to encourage and holds your child accountable. It teaches her the natural consequences of her behavior. Consequences provide boundaries to comfort her from the frightening feeling of her own outbursts and tantrums.

Chapter 12

How to Teach Conflict Resolution

No parent escapes sibling rivalry. Some days my boys seem to intentionally choose to fight. Even if we offered two of the same fire trucks, one would still want the truck that the other one had. And just as I have finally convinced one of them to play with the "less desirable" truck, the other one would make a grab for it, too.

Let's not forget the hitting, the "mine!" and the pestering of one another. Parents have become referees in their own homes!

When my husband and I were expecting for the second time, we wanted our kids to get along, right from the start. We knew they'd disagree (as all people do), but we wanted to teach them how to resolve conflict and grow up to be friends as much as possible.

Because here's the thing: I don't believe constant sibling fighting is the norm. Or that kids are destined to have a meaningful relationship with their siblings only when they've moved out. A peaceful house where kids get along is possible.

Conflict is inevitable, even among siblings who are best of friends. What are some ways to stop siblings from fighting and support conflict resolution instead?

Don't Resolve the Conflict for Your Kids

What's your first reaction when your kids fight? Do you barge in, hoping to put an end to the fighting as quickly as you can? Do you immediately look for the offender or placate the victim?

Try instead *not* to resolve their conflict. Yes, it's uncomfortable watching your kids struggle. We feel compelled to be peacemakers and bring order right away. The problem with resolving their conflict is they don't get to learn from their interaction. You're not able to teach them valuable social skills like waiting, turn-taking, and sharing.

Instead, start by describing what happened and what each child must be feeling ("Both of you seem upset because you both want the teddy bear"). Ask older children what they can do to resolve the conflict where both kids are happy with the result.

Offer younger children options to try ("How about we let John hold the bear for a few minutes, then it'll be Jack's turn next. John, when you're done with the bear, remember to give it to Jack"). Guide your kids to speak and interact peacefully with each other.

Show Empathy to Both Children

Even if one child seems to have done a worse offense, empathize with both kids—they each have their reasons for why they did what they did. Acknowledge this reason without putting judgment on either child. One child's actions may have been wrong (pushing, let's say), but the emotions that led him to do so are still valid (feeling like his little brother was invading his space).

Focusing on who started the fight or made the worse offense is a mistake. With conflict resolution, it doesn't matter who started it. Deep down, no child is the "victim" or "perpetrator" when it comes to sibling rivalry. Both kids have valid reasons to address. Even a child who instigates conflict may be saying he needs help with waiting for his turn or using polite words to ask to play. He needs your guidance and attention just as much as the "victim."

One of the best ways to help with conflict resolution without siding with either child is to narrate what's happening. By describing what had transpired, you're putting words to how each child feels, regardless of who instigated the argument. Both children have valid feelings they need acknowledged and expressed.

So you might say to them, "You're fighting over the car. John, you're upset because Jack is playing with the car you just had. And Jack, you're upset because you thought you could play with the car now that John stopped playing with it."

Validate their emotions by saying what each is likely thinking or feeling. They know they're heard and understood. And even if they don't understand every word you say, you're modeling for them (and any of your other kids who stand to witness) what peaceful conflict resolution looks like.

Don't Tolerate Sibling Bullying

Conflict resolution starts with siblings treating one another with respect. Encourage your kids to speak kindly and respectfully to one another, even when they fight. Explain to your child why being rude or talking back to other children or his siblings is wrong. Say, "We don't talk to one another like that. It hurts other people's feelings." Address your child anytime you hear him say something snappy, sarcastic, or inappropriate.

Sometimes we brush aside our kids' squabbles, mistaking sibling bullying for mere fighting. Don't tolerate your kids talking to one another with disrespect or assume that's just how kids fight. Not only is it disrespectful and enables bad habits, but sibling bullying is an ineffective way to resolve conflict. They don't learn anything productive from constant bickering.

Instead, explain that words and actions can hurt. Children's ego and self-centric frame of mind are still normal for their developmental stage. That's why it's even more important to remind them that careless words and a rude tone of voice can affect others around them. You can say, "I get hurt when you say words like that," or "Your brother got sad when you knocked the ball out of his hand on purpose."

Follow it up by teaching your child how to express himself without being disrespectful. It's normal for your kids to disagree, get frustrated, or feel like things are unfair. What's unacceptable, however, is being disrespectful to others. Show him how to ask for a ball politely, or to trade in another toy in exchange for the ball. He can still express his point of view in a kind way.

And of course, the best way to teach him to be respectful is to model respect yourself. Treat your kids, other adults, and yourself with respect and they'll follow suit.

Suggest Different Ways to Cooperate

Turn taking: Turn-taking is my go-to move when the kids are fighting over the same thing. Certain toys even lend themselves well to back and forth interaction. Encourage them to pass balls to one another, or to take turns going up and down the steps.

We've even had luck with extended turn taking. My eldest was wearing his swim goggles around the house (because you know, five-year-olds!). But then his little brother wanted to wear the goggles as well. I explained, "It's your brother's turn right now. When he's done, he'll give them to you." Then I addressed my five-year-old, "When you're done, make sure to give the goggles to him." If he were to forget, I'd remind him to hand the goggles over so both know I mean my word.

Sharing: Many parents mistakenly assume that providing their children with multiple toys prevents them from fighting. They think giving each of their daughters their own kitchen sets will keep the peace.

Yet scarcity leads to better cooperation. With limited resources, your kids are forced to share and create their own system of turn-taking. When they have too many toys, they miss out on learning to cooperate and instead "mark their territory," refusing to part or share with *their* toys.

Of course, kids can have their own special toys that are strictly theirs. And it's fine to give each child his own soccer ball. But giving individual toys isn't necessary. You can model turn-taking rather than a "That's yours, and this is his" mentality.

Dividing the items: Many toys lend themselves to be shared and divided among many kids: blocks, cars, puzzle pieces. Rather than one child using the whole set, all your kids can play with them. Set aside equal pieces among all of them, such as assigning them 15 blocks each.

Playing together: My eldest got irritated when his little brother tried to play with the guitar he was holding. So I explained to my older son that his little brother wants to learn how to play the guitar from him. I said, "He likes the guitar you're playing with. Why don't you show him how it works? He doesn't know how to play it yet."

Suddenly, he's in teacher mode instead of whiny, get-my-brother-away-from-me mode. I've seen the instant switch when I do this, and it's pretty awesome to see their interaction change. Other examples include having your older child point out the cool features of a toy, or read a book to the younger ones.

Highlight the fun they'll have when they play with each other than if they were to play alone. Just because you only have one of something doesn't mean both kids can't play with it together.

Don't Make the Older Child in Charge

"You're their brother, not their parent," we'll tell our eldest when he tries to exert authority. And while being the older sibling does have its roles, he isn't "in charge" the way parents are. He doesn't get to boss his younger siblings around just because he's older. Instead, he can assume the role of big brother and teach, guide, and play with them. Your older child isn't responsible for watching the younger ones and enforcing the rules.

Separate Your Kids if Needed

You'll have your moments when your kids will want to hit each other in the face. Or they'll cry and cry with no end in sight. In cases like these, separate them so they don't hurt each other. They'll also have a much-needed cool-down time. No point trying to make this a teachable moment when your kids are too upset to listen. Focus on calming them down first, pulling them apart if they need the physical space.

Encourage, but Don't Force, Your Kids to Apologize

Once everyone has calmed down, encourage your kids to say sorry or give each other a hug. Explain that apologizing makes everyone feel better. Keep in mind that often, both kids need to apologize, and not just the offender. Apologizing gives them the closure they need and the cue that says things can go back to normal again.

However, don't force them to say sorry. You'll get a lazy or even sarcastic "sorry" with no genuine intent. Worse, they'll be less likely to say it on their own in the future. If a child refuses to say sorry, let it go and say, "Looks like he's not ready to say sorry yet."

With three kids, I needed to find a way to make sure they got along most of the time. That includes listening to their emotions and empathizing with all children. Teaching them how to express frustration. Showing them how to resolve conflicts through negotiation, turn-taking, and playing as a team. And doing as much as we can to prevent sibling rivalry to begin with. All sibling relationships will have conflict. We can do our best to teach them how to resolve them peacefully.

As you might have guessed, parenting with purpose isn't always the easy way out. It's *hard* to pause and ask "why." It takes practice to change the way we communicate with our kids. And to make parenting even more difficult, we also have to reign in one of the most difficult things to control: our temper.

The next chapter—and the last in part two—focuses on a key ingredient in parenting with purpose: how to do so calmly.

Chapter 13

How to Parent Calmly

You're embarrassed to admit it: you've been losing your temper. Whether recently or for a long time, you've been yelling at your child over every little thing.

You're not alone. Ask any mom, and she'll tell you that losing your temper is one of the worst feelings. We've exploded with rage, called our children names, pulled their arm a little too hard. We've even yelled so much that our voices felt strained afterwards.

You're a ticking bomb and can't seem to control your reactions. You see your child misbehave and you immediately feel yourself "going there," like a volcano ready to erupt. You feel like you *need* to yell just to get it out of your system.

As if losing your temper wasn't bad enough, the remorse you feel in the aftermath is even worse. You wish you could immediately hit "undo" like on a computer—erase the damage and start over. Except you can't, and you feel terrible for what you have just done.

You don't want to keep going like this. Getting angry doesn't help with your child's behavior—the more upset you get, the worse she behaves. Or worse, she's scared of you and how you'll react again.

You're even losing your temper with others, from your spouse to crazy drivers on the street. You're not sure if you're able to control your temper and respond calmly.

Maybe you've vowed, "This time, I will be calm with my child. I promise," only to yell again. Then you feel terrible for losing your temper *and* for breaking your word, time and time again.

The weeks before and after the twins were born, I had no patience for my then-three-year-old. I had gone from raising my voice two *times ever* to taking my anger out on him on a near daily basis. I wasn't exactly the model for parenting ("I write a parenting blog, for crying out loud!" I would regretfully think).

It's so easy to snap back with a sarcastic retort, a harsh punishment, or a raised tone of voice. But we all know parenting calmly and responding—not reacting—is more effective than angry reactions.

No amount of parenting with purpose and intention will work if we feel too upset. That much is clear. So what's the solution? We'll discuss six key concepts for helping you parent without losing your temper:

- Understand the "why"
- Recognize your cues
- Understand your child's development
- Don't expect your child to behave all the time
- Reduce your stress
- Be kind to yourself

Understand the "Why"

We've talked at length about connection and empathy for good reason: understanding why your child acts the way she does makes her behavior seem less offensive. Empathizing with her gives you patience so you don't assume she's up to no good. Maybe you think she should've known better until a closer look shows you that she's simply being a two-year-old. She had a bad day just as everyone else does.

When you only look at your child's behavior, it's easy to assume that's the only problem. You might only see a child who refuses to leave the park or pushed another child out of the way. Yes, not leaving the park and pushing another child are problems, but they indicate other factors that could have contributed to them.

Maybe your child gets upset over little things, from losing a toy to refusing to eat breakfast. But what may seem petty to us (*it's just a toy!*) is real to her. She feels just as terrible for losing a stuffed toy as we would if we had lost our wallet or phone. Asking why she feels upset shows you that her complaints feel as real as your own emotions over losing your beloved items.

And maybe the issues stem even deeper than that. Maybe she's dealing with a new baby sister and can't fathom why her days aren't the same anymore. Or she senses you've been extra busy and distracted when you come home from work. Kids resolve and deal with their emotions in ways that may seem like regression to us. Understanding that they may be trying to resolve deeper issues can help placate the anger we feel.

Recognize Your Cues

We act on cues and habits. After you've put away your toothbrush, you reach for your face soap without thinking about it. Once you're washed up, you reach for your towel, all on autopilot. You've ingrained the habit of brushing your teeth, washing your face, then drying off with a towel. Not doing those steps in that order would seem strange.

Such is the power of habit. When you get angry with your child, you react to triggers that set off your temper. Something happens (cue) and you get upset (habit). Learn the cues and triggers that set you off so you can change and replace the habits that react to them.

Maybe your triggers are the messes your child makes, like plopping her feet on the table from her high chair or your kids fighting over the same toy yet again. Every argument, family, and child is different. Find your triggers. What sets you off before you get angry with her?

Once you determine your triggers, you can better identify them when they happen. You'll also know that once they occur, you tend to react by losing your temper.

For instance, one of my triggers is whining. I will hear that high-pitched, nagging voice and react immediately. Once I realized that whining is a trigger, I was able to spot and identify it before I reacted.

Instead of losing your temper, place a "pause" between the cue and the habit. This can be as simple as taking a deep breath or acknowledging the situation by saying to yourself, "You're fighting over the same toy" or "She's whining." A simple phrase can be all you need to keep you from reacting. And more importantly, that pause between your cue and the reaction you would've had breaks old habits.

Understanding the emotional and physical changes that happen when you see your cue helps you replace one habit (yelling) with another (speaking calmly).

Understand Your Child's Development

Your child's emotions are real, no matter how petty they seem to adults. Her emotions and outbursts are also developmentally normal and even *desirable*.

She has and will continue to test her boundaries. She's learning right from wrong. She wants to assert herself and understand her limits. She's also learning how to manage her emotions as well as developing the skills to do so. You *want* her to assert herself and use defiance in a healthy way.

Imagine if your child obeyed every single thing you told her to do. No questions, no resistance, just does everything she's supposed to. It'd be pretty weird, right? You wouldn't want her to be an adult who couldn't stand up for herself or just does everything other people tell her to do.

Accept and even embrace your child's temperament, outbursts, and standoffs. In most cases, kids don't act up to get us angry. They don't *like* feeling upset. They're handling their emotions in the only ways they know how to. They don't have the tools to handle the different scenarios and emotions they're experiencing just yet.

Don't Expect Your Child to Behave All the Time

My five-year-old surprised me when I took him to his first swimming class. Having long been afraid of the water, he powered through class, taking on challenges I hadn't expected him to.

"Don't worry," I reassured him at the end of class. "That's as hard as it gets."

Little did I know I would bite my own words. In the second swim class, I thought he would plug on through just as he did the first time. Except he didn't: he refused to go in the water, crying and drawing attention from the crowd. Nothing the coaches or I said convinced him to give it a try. He rebuffed every suggestion I made to get in the water.

And when I agreed to go home, he claimed he wanted to swim. Clearly his emotions had taken over, and no logic or reason could get through.

Where was my little trooper who overcame his fears last week? He behaved so well during the first class. I felt more frustrated that he had done well the first time only to throw a tantrum the second time around.

This isn't the first time I felt this way, either. For instance, I've been impatient with my kids for crying at family parties when in the past, they had been social and friendly. "Why are they crying now when they were totally fine the last time?" I'd think.

Then I realized that just because kids behaved well in the past, they won't always do so in the future. They'll have off days just as you and I do. Think about it: you're patient with your child, right? But you also have days when you're not exactly on your A-game.

Sometimes because our child is normally so well-behaved, we get upset when she isn't. "Shouldn't she know better by now?" you might ask. But we all have bad days, including our kids. A perfect track record in the past doesn't mean you or your child are guaranteed perfect days in the future.

Reduce Your Stress

Have you lashed out at your child not because you were mad at her, but because you were mad at something or someone else? If you're like me, you've taken your frustration out on your kids rather than deal with the issues or people you'd rather not confront.

Your temper could easily rise from factors that have nothing to do with your child, from a fight with your partner to an ever-growing workload. Your stress can even stem from something small, like trying to fix the Internet while your child is asking you to find her sippy cup. Parenting mindfully is difficult when stress factors stand in your way.

For smaller scale stress factors, you can make simple changes, like fixing the Internet when your child is napping. Recognizing your stress triggers can be enough to keep you from yelling.

Larger stress factors might need more introspection and perhaps equally large changes in your life. Whether you're able to make those changes or not, being aware of your stress factors will at least help you realize that some of your frustration stems not from your child but from other parts of your life.

Be Kind to Yourself

Let's not forget one very important side in the parent-child relationship: yours. For however much you focus on your child's emotions and growth, pay attention to your own as well.

Because let's be real: parenting calmly doesn't mean enjoying your child's tantrums or suppressing your own frustrations. Being calm doesn't mean separating yourself from your emotions or pretending they don't exist.

Instead of exploding or suppressing your frustration, acknowledge them. Just as you would tell your child, "Looks like you're upset," acknowledge *your* emotions too. Admit that it gets hard sometimes. You'd rather have a good time with your child instead of console her through another tantrum. You're tired of dealing with her crying for the fifth time today.

Remember, you're doing a good job. We don't say that to ourselves enough. You're committed to doing your best in this parenting journey. Don't forget that. Validating your feelings brings you back to the calm you need to parent effectively.

None of these tips are easy. They're certainly not shortcuts. You're taking extra steps to stop your anger and redirect your child to something more productive. And you're doing so when she's at her worst. Practicing any of these calming measures won't result in warm and fuzzy feelings. Sometimes it can even feel unnatural (who wants to keep their voice calm when her child is yelling?).

But you don't want to continue yelling. Losing your temper feels draining and exhausting. And you know a better alternative is out there.

Parenting mindfully keeps you from raising your voice and opens your eyes to a potential learning moment. Yelling at your child can sometimes "work": she'll obey, be quiet and leave you alone. But it doesn't solve the long-term problem or teach her how to cope next time. Yelling can happen again and more often, or worse, erect a wall between the two of you.

Instead, use these heated events as teachable moments. Both you and your child learn patience, respect, and empathy.

For instance, find what's causing her to act up—she's probably not doing something to get you upset. Maybe she needs you to redirect her to a more appropriate activity. You may even realize that her behavior stems from something deeper. She could be going through scary changes or new developmental milestones she still needs to work on.

Through connection, you recognize your triggers and cues. Think about all those times you've gotten upset at your child. What happened right before you exploded? Find your triggers, whether it's whining, your kids fighting, or feeling rushed to get out the house. Maybe you're trying to do something else and she's clamoring for your attention.

Find ways to replace your habits with a more effective response. If your previous habit was to yell, maybe now you take a breath, close your eyes, or say, "I'm getting mad." This extra pause turns your reaction into a response that doesn't include yelling.

And remember, your child's tantrums or stubbornness, however unpleasant, are actually normal and *desirable*. You want her to assert herself instead of being an obedient drone. All kids test their boundaries.

And they have bad days, like you and me. Your child has been a champ with feeding herself, but her track record doesn't mean she won't spill her food once in a while. Try not to lose your temper because she couldn't keep it together that day.

Focus on yourself as well. Reduce the stress in your life that contribute to your temper and ask yourself what you're frustrated about. Do you take your anger out on your child when you're actually frustrated at someone or something? Do you snap at her to be quiet when you're trying to get stuff done around the house? Has your overscheduled calendar led to disconnection with your family? Take a look at life changes, both big and small, that you may need to make to keep you from feeling overwhelmed.

And lastly, be kind to yourself. This is a hard job! The more you learn about yourself and your kids, the better your relationship. You'll have less conflict, and you'll be able to deal with them effectively when they happen.

Chapter 13 - How to Parent Calmly

This concludes the second part of the book. Part one outlined new habits that prevent outbursts. Part two discussed how to deal with them when they happen. Now, in part three, we'll talk about what to do *after* the outbursts and what we can learn from them.

PART THREE

THE POST-CONFLICT ACTION PLAN

Chapter 14

Why You Don't Need to Discipline Immediately

How do you react when you're about to discipline your child? If you're like me, these two mistakes will sound all too familiar:

One, you use the moment to teach your child about the various lessons he can learn. You emphasize that hitting others is not acceptable. You point out how the other child must feel hurt, or how words are better to communicate his frustrations. You want the "teachable moment" to stick before time runs out and you lose the opportunity.

Or two, you react with anger or annoyance. You discipline immediately, laying out the consequences, holding your ground, standing firm. Or worse, you lose your temper, too frustrated to even deal with the moment, much less make it a teachable one.

But each scenario disregards the time you and your child may need to calm down. Jumping in too quickly to redirect or teach may not be taking into account his disposition. Trying to teach a frustrated, scared or sad child a lesson, especially when *we're* upset, is ineffective.

The most effective time to hold a discussion with your child is when you're *both* calm. Don't lecture, teach or give consequences when he's whining or being stubborn.

Your first agenda isn't to give consequences, especially if you're upset. Connect first. Express empathy for your child's feelings, often without words. Hold him close until his crying dies down to mere hiccups and sniffles.

Don't jump the gun to lay out the consequences. Instead consider yourself on the same side as him, not the opposite.

You can't get through to your child if he is too upset to listen. During heightened emotions, he isn't able to see reason. He isn't receptive to the best parenting techniques. Instead, he feels "fight or flight" emotions—the same you'd feel during road rage, for instance. He's reacting based on anger and defensiveness, not logic or reason.

Trying to teach when either of you are angry or upset is ineffective and a waste of time. Your child won't learn a lesson. Instead he'll get angrier, escalating emotions even further.

The next time you or your child feel upset, wait. It's *really* okay to just wait until you're both calm. If you're upset, explain to him, "I'm upset right now, so I need to go to my room to calm down for a minute." If he feels upset, acknowledge his emotions. Hold him close or stay nearby, comforting him with a back rub or sitting him on your lap. You can even wait until the next day to discuss his actions.

Your waiting period can be as quick as a short breath. That one pause is enough to separate the trigger from the reaction. Then once you've paused, label your emotion. Either in your head or out loud, say, "I feel mad." Notice the physical changes in your body, from a faster heartbeat to tensing muscles. The acknowledgment forces you to choose whether to remain mad or calm down. Simply reacting doesn't even give you that choice.

Sometimes the best thing to do is to let your child be and leave him alone. He may be too upset to talk or listen. Don't reason or discipline, either, since he can't process anything you're saying in that state.

Waiting until your child calms down is much faster than going straight into discipline mode or getting upset. The more upset you are, the more upset he will be. And disciplining him when he's throwing a tantrum is going to make him feel even worse.

But waiting until the right opportunity? Connection is an instant release of his pent-up emotions. I've seen this with my own kids. I kneel beside them and show empathy towards their feelings (misbehavior or not). And I can see them shed their defensiveness. They shrug off the tough guy act, bury their faces in my arms and release their tears.

Had I not done that—had I disciplined or scolded immediately— they would've taken longer to calm down. They'd have to bottle their emotions or resist any teachable moment I may have been trying to get through. Any sort of parenting or disciplining would've fallen on deaf ears.

My kids calm down much faster when I say, "Mama's here. You can cry to me," than when I lose my temper or teach a lesson. They know I'm on their side ready to help.

Because the best time to teach your child what he can learn from that moment is when you're both calm. Discipline is teaching, and you'd want him to learn when he's in the best mindset to do so. You also can't teach if *you're* too upset.

When do you know you're ready to discuss? When your child has stopped crying and has started talking. When you can think of a logical consequence and can articulate it without judgment. When you're ready to respond and not simply react.

Take a breath, pause, don't talk. Focus on empathizing and calming him down first. And when you're both ready, begin the important step of discussing emotions as outlined in the next chapter.

Chapter 15

The Importance of Discussing Emotions

Many of the challenges with our kids stem from their inability to comprehend emotions the way you and I do. Kids can't always define why they feel cloudy or why their body feels different with each emotion. And so they act up, withdraw, or hit instead of communicate. They don't know any better.

Your child isn't born with the ability to discern emotions, especially unpleasant ones. She knows something different is happening, both physically and mentally, but she has no idea what's going on. She might think this unpleasant feeling is permanent. Or she might feel terrified, not knowing why these feelings are happening. She might also wonder whether she's the only one who has experienced this feeling.

That is, until you define these emotions, like "mad" or "worried" or "sad." Highlight more pleasant feelings of pride, excitement, and joy as well. As your child begins to build her repertoire of emotions, she learns that feelings come and go. That feelings don't define her—she *feels* bad, she's not a bad person. And she learns to cope with feelings and learn that everyone goes through them at some point.

You and I have had plenty of years to identify emotions. From joy to jealousy, anger to excitement, we know the feelings we have. We know they'll pass, even if in hindsight. And we know we're not the only ones who experience emotions. Everyone goes through them as well. Our kids are still learning these emotions.

Words are powerful. Labeling emotions helps your child claim control over sadness, jealousy, fear. She may not be able to articulate that her heart is clenching or her head hurting. She may not understand why she'd rather be by herself than do fun things. To say, "It looks like you feel sad," helps her identify sadness and, more importantly, reassures her that she's not alone in feeling this way.

The more you label and discuss emotions, the better behaved your child will act. For one thing, she can better identify emotions through words when she knows which ones to use. She can better communicate her feelings without resorting to physical expression. Your toddler can say, "I'm mad!" rather than hit her brother out of anger.

She'll also understand that feelings don't define her. She can feel grumpy without believing she's a grumpy girl all the time. She won't assume she must be a bad person because she keeps getting upset and throwing daily tantrums. She knows emotions come and go and don't last forever.

Labeling and discussing emotions also tell your child that you love her no matter what emotions she happens to feel. You'll never withhold your affection because she's being unpleasant. Or that she has to be happy to get your attention.

And finally, talking about emotions helps tap into your child's logical side. She's just experienced some pretty chaotic emotions. Just a few minutes ago, she wouldn't even have been able to process anything you tried to tell her. Labeling emotions puts order to the chaos.

What are some of the ways to discuss emotions with your child?

As she's calming down, begin by saying, "You seem mad," as you hold her in your arms. Hearing the words identify what she's feeling will calm her down much faster than putting her in time-out or getting upset.

Once she's calm and receptive, discuss her emotions further. First, admit you've felt the same way she does. Discuss a time, whether in your current life or when you were her age, when you've felt upset. You're empathizing and placing yourself on the same side once more.

Then, explain that everyone has felt the same way as well. She isn't alone or strange for feeling the way she does. Empathize by honoring the impulse: "It must've been frustrating when he knocked down your tower of blocks. I'd feel pretty upset too if that happened to me." Or correct the behavior, and empathize and label the emotion: "It looks like you're feeling tired and sad. But I can't let you pull on the curtains because they could break. Let's look for something else to pull."

Discuss the changes she might feel in her body during those heightened emotions. Explain how our hearts beat faster when we're upset, or that our bodies feel tight, and sometimes our head hurts. She'll begin to recognize the symptoms of her emotions.

And finally, suggest different ways she can cope with her emotions. Discuss what she can do to deal with her feelings. For instance, if her brother knocked down the blocks, she can come to you for help. She can say, "I'm mad" or grab her special blanket. Or maybe she can go to her room to color and calm down. Older kids can even brainstorm ways to cope with their emotions and what will help make them feel better.

Helping your child through a tantrum or resolving a standoff is one thing. Learning how to best cope with it is another. Sure, you could calm her down and leave it at that, but you lose the opportunity for her to learn. The better equipped she'll be to cope with emotions, the less outbursts she'll have. Now, rather than reacting, she can better identify her emotions and regulate them.

Begin labeling emotions, from happy to sad to angry and the others between. The more your child is able to place a name on a feeling, the quicker she'll identify the feeling by word, not in a vague outburst or retort.

Because if you're like me, one of the ways you feel better about a bad day is by talking or writing about it. Often I do both. I'll question something I did that day, for instance, but in talking to my husband, I feel loads better. I could see the logic in my actions. That everyone goes through emotions like frustration or embarrassment. And that it may not be as bad as I imagined.

Perhaps the best part of discussing the aftermath of your child's behavior is the bonding between you both. You'll further deepen the trust she has placed in you when you empathize with her emotions. She'll feel safe sitting next to you as you both unveil the frustrations that just transpired. You forge a stronger connection when you admit your faults as well as brainstorm ways to resolve them.

Chapter 16

Self-Reflection: What You Can Learn in the Aftermath

Parenting with purpose instills lifelong lessons for both you and your child. Yes, on a daily basis your goals may be, "I just want my child to brush his teeth without putting up a fight," or "I want him to listen the first time without nagging."

But for parenthood to be truly meaningful and effective, one-time solutions don't cut it. You want to build a long-term, close relationship with your child. You want parenting to get easier—and yes, it *can* get easier. You want to teach important values and learn lessons you can both carry with you moving forward.

This is why parenting with purpose is so important. You're not just reacting to your child's latest antics and trying to get him to stop. You're intentional about what you want to happen. You're aware of what's going on so you don't react—you respond according to him and the situation. And you help him develop life skills so that the same issue doesn't keep coming up over and over again.

I get how difficult it can be to maintain that consistently. You're rushing out the door to get to school on time. Your other child won't stop crying because she can't find her shoe, and the baby has been up all night with colic. You're not always thinking about parenting with purpose. In those crazy moments, you just want your baby to stop crying, your child to find her shoe, and for everyone to leave the house on time. We all go through those days, no exceptions. Day-to-day parenting can be hectic.

But in parenting with purpose, you find more opportunities to analyze yourself, your children, and that particular situation. You build skills so that the day-to-day hassles don't pile up. And when they do, you don't react so quickly but rather are more definitive in your responses. Your mornings run smoothly. And you're then better able to focus on helping your children thrive.

How?

Successful parenthood depends on reflecting and learning from the moment. You might see your child's outbursts repeat or escalate if you don't think about the factors that played a role in it; the things that could've gone better or triggered it in the first place.

Once all is calm, ask yourself what you learned. Take a look at some questions you might ask yourself after your child's outburst:

- **What were the triggers?** What caused your child to act up? Triggers can be as simple as wanting to stay at the park, to more complex such as feeling anxious about starting the new school year.

- **What is your child's temperament?** Understanding his temperament can determine how well you interact with him. You may have assumptions of how he should act based on your personality, or his siblings'. Instead, think about your child's general temperament (I say "general" because as we all know, everyone acts a little differently from day to day). Work with his temperament rather than change it.

- **What were the circumstances?** Sometimes, the environment led to your child's behavior. Did he have a meltdown about not being able to play with the remote controls? Keep them out of his reach to avoid future battles over remote controls.

Or maybe you learned large crowds overwhelm him. Taking him to the large carnival in the middle of the day when he's hungry might not work, but leaving first thing in the morning after a snack just might.

- **How is your home environment?** Other times, our children act in response to our home environment. For instance, an overscheduled family life without down time can tire your child and lead him to whine or act extra grumpy. Or maybe the lack of routines has led him to feel anxious and scared.

- **What was *your* disposition before and during the outburst?** I'll admit, sometimes I get distracted. Either I'm looking at my phone and lose my patience with my kids because they "interrupted" me, or I've got things on my mind and can't focus on them. I've succumbed to losing my patience during those situations. My anger then made their outbursts worse than had I been more mindful and present.

Discuss the conflict with another adult as well. Talk to your partner, a close friend, or your childcare providers to get their opinion. Work with other adults and caregivers to see if they've noticed a similar pattern. Ask them what they recommend. Make sure adults who interact with your child regularly are on the same page as you so he isn't confused by inconsistency.

And remember, don't take your child's misbehavior too personally. We think our children crying must mean we're failing somehow or that others think the worst when we yell at our kids in public. We've all felt the same way and regretted actions we wished we could take back. While we can strive to improve our parenting, no one would ever get 100% on this parenting business.

Don't feel terrible about what you did or didn't do, or what you could've or shouldn't have done. Don't cloud your mind with blame.

Assess your interaction with your child, learn from it, and be proactive instead. Feeling ashamed isn't productive to anyone.

Parenting success isn't winning battles with your child or getting him to obey you all the time. You want to reduce misbehavior, but expecting complete obedience isn't reasonable or desirable. Don't think of conflict with him as winning or losing. You're not a failure because the tantrum lasted a whole hour (in public, no less!).

Instead, think about what to learn. Mistakes can be some of our best teachers. Consider each behavior as another learning opportunity to do even better in the future.

Look at the conflict with your child through different angles. Discuss them with other people. Then think about what changes to make. What can you do to meet his developmental challenges? For instance, say he's going through a typical tantrum stage. What can you do to lessen them in the first place? Practice handling tantrums to better connect with your child at their level. Use connection and empathy rather than reason to get through to him.

Maybe you realized you've been too lenient and now have to put your foot down gently but firmly. Think about the goals you want for your child and the challenges that can stand in his way. Learn how to follow through with logical consequences or accommodate flexibility into your consistent rules.

You won't know this without the necessary self-reflection after each incident. This is where the real learning happens. Learn about your family and the ways to connect with your child, even during conflicts. Parent with purpose to establish lifelong skills for both you and your child.

PARENTING WITH PURPOSE

Parenting is an ongoing process and never complete. Reading every piece of parenting advice won't stop your children from misbehaving.

But you're reading this. You want to improve your parenting. You're aware of yourself, your child, and the factors that contribute to outbursts. When you parent with purpose, outbursts will lessen and get easier. How?

For one, you will be more attuned to your child. You know what sets her off and what helps her thrive. You prevent outbursts to begin with because you know her well and how to help her cope with her emotions.

Second, your child will be more attuned to herself. With you guiding her through her emotions, she has a better grasp of feelings and how to cope with them. She knows she can go to her room when she's overwhelmed with a crowd. Or that she can grab her special blanket to calm down. With each outburst, she improves the skills to regulate her emotions.

Third, parenting with purpose meets your child's needs. She doesn't feel empty for affection because you've given her your full attention. She knows she's loved even if she may have done something wrong. She doesn't worry you'll leave her or that you'd only spend time with her when she's happy. With her emotional needs met, she'll be less likely to act up.

And lastly, you will have established ground rules for your child. By being consistent with rules and responsibilities, you define clear expectations without nagging.

You also accommodate flexibility into your lives to accommodate life's uncertainties. Balancing consistency and flexibility gives her the space to explore, but within boundaries. She knows where she's safe to explore, and when to hold back.

Through this book, you've learned a new definition of discipline. Discipline is not just about punishment or time-outs or even giving consequences.

Discipline is teaching your child how to regulate her emotions and label feelings and to better communicate and act with respect. You teach her to be the person—and the adult—you hope she becomes.

And you do this through connection. Rather than creating a divide when your child needs you the most, you draw her in. Through her tantrums and outbursts, you show her you've got her back and love her no matter what. You respect her the way you'd want her to treat you and others. And you realize you're on the same—not opposing—sides.

Misbehavior and outbursts are inevitable. After all, that's how children test and learn their limits. Even we adults have bad days and throw tantrums too. But we've gotten better, and so will your child.

The more she can regulate her emotions, the fewer outbursts you'll see. The fuller her bucket is, the less she'll resort to antics to get your attention.

Dealing with heavy emotions and unpleasant situations is never easy. No parent looks forward to another tantrum. But through connection, you will be better attuned to your child. You won't take it personally or react with anger each time.

You'll know the best ways to comfort your child and the best time to discipline. Both of you will be better equipped to handle conflict.

Parenting is a difficult yet fulfilling job. You go from surviving the day-to-day to helping your child grow and mature. You'll build a strong parent-child relationship now, and well into the future.

20 Actionable Items You Can Do

Phew.

You've just read a whole lot of information on parenting. Any changes you plan to make aren't exactly as clear-cut as opening a savings account or organizing your home. Parenting depends on your child, any particular moment, and other life circumstances.

No wonder there isn't a one-size-fits-all strategy.

It's easy to feel like you don't know where to start. You have so much information in your head, not just from this book but from other resources you've found. Keeping track of what you're supposed to do and when and in what way is challenging. It's overwhelming thinking about all the things you could be doing.

Even with all the resources at your fingertips, no one does it all. You can read the best parenting advice and *still* make mistakes. That's what makes us human. No matter how many times we tell ourselves to respect our kids, we still end up bossing them around. We vow yet again not to yell, and somehow we still do. Nobody's perfect, including you and me.

And that's why doing even just *one* thing is better than thinking we're doomed to bad parenting, or that our kids are simply this way with little to do to salvage our relationship with them. We don't have to stick it out until they grow out of it (only to get into another challenging phase later on).

So I summarized the key points of this book into 20 actionable items you can do. Some of these you can actually plan ahead of time. For instance, one of them encourages you to greet your child with genuine joy when you first see him (from part one about connecting).

Other action plans are meant to keep in mind if or when the situation calls for it. For instance, I advise you to hold your ground against his unnecessary demands. These are goals to focus on if or when they happen.

The goal of this section is for you to take action, even if you focus on just one thing. Maybe you do one thing every day. Or one thing for several weeks until it feels natural. The order is unimportant. Focus on whichever you feel is easiest or most necessary to start.

Take a look through this action plan when you feel overwhelmed with advice or don't know where to start. As you'll see, even little steps can make a big difference.

#1: Give your child a responsibility.
Your child will rise to your expectations. When you set them low, coddle too much, or doubt his abilities, he'll perform accordingly. Instead, give him responsibilities one notch more challenging than what he's used to. The responsibility isn't so difficult that he feels discouraged and frustrated, but challenging enough to make him feel important and valued.

Maybe this means using the same dishes adults in your home use instead of the plastic ones. Entrusting him to make his bed every morning. Putting away the groceries.

Meanwhile, focus on changing your own assumptions about your child. Even if he makes mistakes (breaks a dish one of the days, for instance), realize that everyone does from time to time. Help him fix the mistake and learn from it. But don't use the potential of mistakes as a barrier from challenging him in the future.

#2: Offer your child a choice.

Think of a challenging part of your day. Maybe that's getting out the door in the morning or convincing your child to eat his dinner. Instead of dreading the predictable struggle, offer him two parent-approved choices.

If your child stalls getting out the door, state the fact ("We're leaving in a few minutes"). Then offer two parent-approved choices ("Do you want to bring your book or your dinosaur?").

#3: Light up your face when you reunite with your child.

From greeting him in the morning to picking him up at school, reunite with your child in a positive way. Make your face light up like you are so excited to see him rather than a nod and a lackluster "hey there."

He hasn't seen you in a while (and yes, the hours asleep at night are still, in his eyes, time apart from you). Start your time together off on a positive note by showing him how happy you are to see him.

Don't overdo this to the point where it seems fake—a grand affair could feel overwhelming and old after a while. Instead, feel glad to see him, give him a warm hug, smile wide, and let your eyes do the talking.

#4: Spend five to ten minutes with your child without interruptions.

Want to avoid your child clamoring for your attention at the most inconvenient times? Carve out 5—10 minutes to focus on him. Avoid other tasks like wiping the table or checking your phone while spending time with him: devote time with him doing whatever he wants to do.

The few minutes of focusing your attention on your child will fill his bucket and make him less needy and whiny later on.

#5: Praise your child's positive behavior.
Despite his misbehavior, your child has done something worth praising. From reading a book on his own to treating his brother kindly, these are positive actions you can praise. Kids respond much better with positive praise than being reprimanded for negative behavior. The more you praise him for behaving well, the more he'll continue that behavior.

#6: Create a daily schedule.
If your days feel like they have no structure, create a daily schedule to stick to. Base your activities on two main pillars: eating and sleeping. Consider when you want your child to eat for breakfast, lunch, dinner, and snacks. Then write when naptimes and bedtimes occur in your home.

Now that you've got your basics down, you can create smaller routines, like brushing teeth before taking a bath or putting toys away at the end of the day.

#7: Implement habits your child can do.
Routines and habits help your child go through the day without nagging. Create consistent habits such as having your child eat at the same place and roughly the same time. When you announce the food is ready, he'll know exactly where to go. Create a habit of brushing his teeth at 6:45pm every night, with bath time right after. You won't have to remind him what comes next.

Schedules and habits help your child feel grounded and comforted. He can focus on playing rather than feeling anxious over what comes next. And he will likely comply much more when he expects these habits and routines.

#8: Speak just as respectfully to your child as you would another adult.

Ever feel like we just boss our kids around? Problem is, we probably do, and it doesn't sound nice to their ears. Think about what you say to your child. Reconsider whether you would say that to another adult or someone you respect.

So avoid the bossiness, the yelling, the curt and rude comments. You can still be firm when establishing rules, but do so respectfully.

#9: Describe, don't demand.

If you see something your child has neglected, describe it. "Your socks are on the floor." Starting with this technique can deflect power struggles. He's more likely to put his socks away if it isn't a demand. You might have luck starting with this method first before explicitly telling him the tasks he should've done.

#10: Ask yourself why your child did what he did.

The next time your child doesn't behave well, don't assume he has done something on purpose, out of mischief or to spite you. Think about *why* he did it instead. Often the reason is an honest one and not rooted in intentional misbehavior. Other times he may have forgotten the rules or can't contain himself.

Say your child was reaching over the edge of the bed, scaring you into thinking he might fall over. Before you think he was up to no good, ask yourself why he was doing that. You'll realize his intentions are usually innocent, like reaching over to get a book.

#11: Empathize with your child.

When your child feels upset, express that you understand how he must feel. Show empathy by sharing a time when you felt the same way, either when you were his age or now as an adult.

Empathy is one of the best relationship-building tools between parent and child. Putting yourself in another person's shoes places both of you on the same, not opposing sides. And it teaches him how to express empathy and use it to understand others around him.

#12: Redirect your child's behavior to a similar appropriate activity.

Not all actions are terrible. While throwing a tennis ball indoors may not be appropriate, throwing it outside is. Throwing itself isn't a terrible action. You just need to redirect him to a more appropriate activity or setting.

The same can be said with how your child communicates. If he talks back or says something rudely, ask him to phrase it nicely instead.

#13: Speak to your child at or below eye level.

One of the best ways to calm or comfort your child is by getting at or below his eye level. Speaking to him standing above makes him feel threatened and cowered. But at his level, he lets go of his defenses and feels like you're on his side.

I've had better luck calming my kids down when I've put myself at eye level with them. They feel less defensive and are more willing to let me comfort them.

#14: Follow through with logical consequences.

Hold your child accountable for his actions by following through with consequences. He'll learn that his choices have repercussions, both good and bad. And remember that the consequences need to tie in logically to his behavior.

#15: Hold your ground.

Focus on holding your ground if you feel like your child needs boundaries. This doesn't mean you're strict or rigid. Think about your priorities, what you want to teach, and the values you want to impart.

Children need guidance and boundaries within which to explore. If left free to roam, they will have no one to teach them right or wrong. Kids feel scared when their emotions run rampant. If their own parents can't stand up to their tantrums and shrink at each outburst, then who will?

#16: When comforting your child, don't say anything.

We get so tempted to teach and lecture when our children feel upset. Except if your child isn't receptive, nothing you say is getting through. Save that for another time. Instead, hold him, rub his back, rock him side to side, and at most, say, "I know," or "It hurts, doesn't it?"

At this stage, your child doesn't need to learn a lesson, and certainly not a lecture. The more you comfort your child with empathy, the quicker and more receptive he will be to any teachable moments you want to convey.

#17: Apologize to your child.

We're not infallible. Many times we've wished we could retract harsh words or hasty actions. Perhaps we were angry with our kids, or we yelled a little too hard to get them out of a tantrum. We can't undo our mistakes; there's no way to rewind and change what's done. Instead, we do the next best thing: apologize.

Apologizing to your child is important for so many reasons. You let him know that you make mistakes just as much as he does.

You teach him *how* to say sorry. You respect him enough to admit when you need his forgiveness. Apologizing humbles you to empathize and see things from his perspective.

#18: Label emotions.
Whether your child feels happy, sad, or angry, point out his emotions. Say how excited he must be feeling, getting to blow out his birthday cake. Or how happy he made his brother when he helped him fix a toy.

Help define other unpleasant feelings he might have as well like sadness, anger, jealousy, or anxiety. You can state it as a question, "Are you a little nervous about your first day of school?"

#19: Define and say your trigger.
Find out what leads you to lose your temper with your child. Is it when your kids are fighting over the same toy? When he's whining? When he's talking like a two-year-old (and he's going on six)? The triggers can be anything, whether legitimate or silly. Learn what sets you off before you react.

When you do spot the trigger, repeat it, either out loud or to yourself: "He's whining," or "He's talking like a two-year-old." The act of saying your trigger builds a pause between your child's action and your reaction, encouraging you to respond, not react.

#20: Reflect on your day.
Whether good or bad, think about your day and what has transpired. What connection-building activities worked well? What could you do better? What were the circumstances that led to the outburst? Learn about your child and yourself to build a strong parent-child relationship.

Resources

For more information, visit Sleeping Should Be Easy:
www.sleepingshouldbeeasy.com

Further reading:

- *Becoming the Parent You Want to Be* by Laura Davis
- *Taking Back Childhood* by Nancy Carlsson-Paige
- *The Whole Brain Child* by Daniel J. Siegel and Tina Payne Bryson
- *No-Drama Discipline* by Daniel J. Siegel and Tina Payne Bryson
- *The Power of Positive Parenting* by Glenn Latham
- *The Bright Kid Challenge* by Andrew Fuller
- *All Joy and No Fun* by Jennifer Senior
- *Peaceful Parent, Happy Kids* by Laura Markham
- *Daring Greatly* by Brené Brown
- *Mindset* by Carol Dweck
- *NurtureShock* by Po Bronson
- *Hold On to Your Kids* by Gabor Maté

Get my ebook, FREE!

Feeling overwhelmed with parenthood?

I'd love to share some of my best material with you in my ebook, *Time Management Strategies for the Overwhelmed Mom*, when you subscribe to my newsletter. This 28-page ebook is chock-full of practical tips and advice on how to feel less overwhelmed.

You'll also receive exclusive weekly parenting tips and giveaways you won't find on the blog. No spam ever, and you can unsubscribe at any time.

Go to **sleepingshouldbeeasy.com/list** to get your free ebook!

10161163R00072

Printed in Great Britain
by Amazon